BizTalk 2013 EDI for Supply Chain Management

Working with Invoices, Purchase Orders, and Related Document Types

Mark Beckner

Apress·

BizTalk 2013 EDI for Supply Chain Management: Working with Invoices, Purchase Orders and Related Document Types

An Apress Advanced Book

Copyright © 2013 by Mark Beckner

ISBN 978-1-4302-6343-2

ISBN 978-1-4302-6344-9 (eBook)

President and Publisher: Paul Manning
Lead Editor: Steve Weiss
Editorial Board: Steve Anglin, Ewan Buckingham, Gary Cornell, Louise Corrigan, Jonathan Gennick, Jonathan Hassell, Robert Hutchinson, Michelle Lowman, James Markham, Matthew Moodie, Jeff Olson, Jeffrey Pepper, Douglas Pundick, Ben Renow-Clarke, Dominic Shakeshaft, Gwenan Spearing, Matt Wade, Steve Weiss, Tom Welsh
Coordinating Editor: Anamika Panchoo
Copy Editor: Mary Behr
Compositor: SPi Global
Indexer: Kumar Dhaneesh
Artist: SPi Global
Cover Designer: Anna Ishchenko

Distributed to the book trade worldwide by Springer Science+Business Media New York, 233 Spring Street, 6th Floor, New York, NY 10013. Phone 1-800-SPRINGER, fax (201) 348-4505, e-mail orders-ny@springer-sbm.com, or visit www.springeronline.com.

For information on translations, please e-mail rights@apress.com, or visit www.apress.com.

Apress and friends of ED books may be purchased in bulk for academic, corporate, or promotional use. eBook versions and licenses are also available for most titles. For more information, reference our Special Bulk Sales–eBook Licensing web page at www.apress.com/bulk-sales.

Contents at a Glance

Contents

About the Author

Mark Beckner is a technical consultant specializing in business strategy and enterprise application integration. He runs his own consulting firm, Inotek Consulting Group, LLC, delivering innovative solutions to large corporations and small businesses. His projects have included engagements with numerous clients throughout the U.S., and range in nature from mobile application development to complete integration solutions. He has authored *BizTalk 2010 EDI for Health Care*, *BizTalk 2010 Recipes*, *Pro EDI in BizTalk Server 2006 R2*, and *Pro RFID in BizTalk Server 2009*, and has spoken at a number of venues, including Microsoft TechEd. In addition to BizTalk, he works with Microsoft Dynamics CRM, SharePoint, and custom .NET development. Beckner, his wife, Sara, and his boys, Ciro and Iyer, live somewhere in the rugged deserts and/or mountains of the American West. His web site is www.inotekgroup.com, and he can be contacted directly at mbeckner @inotekgroup.com.

About the Author

Introduction

BizTalk is a development platform and lends itself to a wide variety of implementation styles. After you've worked with the platform on a number of projects, however, you will find that there are really only a few patterns that meet the critical requirements of a well-developed solution. With every project, you must ask the following questions:

1. Do I have all of the requirements, and is the business communicating the correct requirements to me?

2. Is there a way to architect this solution that will ensure I have the simplest set of components required to successfully deliver?

3. Will I be able to easily communicate how to work with this to someone else?

4. Is my solution maintainable and supportable?

The examples outlined in this book are intended to give you a pattern on which to build your own implementations. They outline the common tasks that will be encountered on virtually any EDI project, and they also show some unique approaches to solving complex problems. Most importantly, they demonstrate that BizTalk EDI solutions can be simple and fairly quick to implement.

My hope is that this book will aid you in realizing success with your own projects.

Contacting the Author

If you have questions regarding the concepts in this book, or would like to discuss architecture, mentoring, or development options, please contact me at `mbeckner @inotekgroup.com`.

Solution: Receiving850Da ta

This chapter will walk through a complete end-to-end solution on how to build out BizTalk to receive 850 (Purchase Order) documents from an external trading partner and send an acknowledgement back. The data will be received via an SFTP adapter and then it will be archived and processed by an orchestration. In the orchestration, it will be determined whether the purchase order needs to be reviewed manually by an internal user prior to approval, or whether it can be delivered automatically as a flat file to the internal order processing application. This will introduce many of the key concepts required in working with inbound data.

The data will be received in unencrypted format on an SFTP site, will be archived by a BizTalk orchestration using a .NET library, and will be mapped to a flat file format. The rules determining whether the data can be automatically approved, or whether it required manual approval, will be handled in the orchestration, but additional ideas on how to make this more robust will be presented at the end of this chapter. The overview of this specific solution is shown in Figure 1-1.

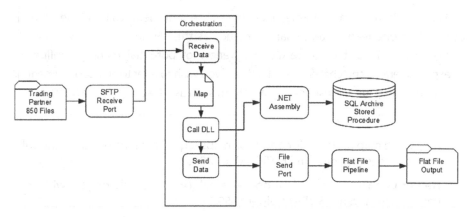

Figure1 -1. Inbound 850 solution overview

Visual Studio Solution

It is critical that your project structure and namespaces are correct from the start. If these are not exactly what you need for the proper architecture and organization of your solution, you'll be spending a great deal of time later in the process rewriting and retesting. For this solution, the namespace is in a structure that you should be able to use directly within your own solutions, substituting the wording, but not the structure. You will also be creating a Visual Studio project structure that will be generic enough to fit within any model you may encounter. In the case of the solution being built out, the following Visual Studio projects and namespaces will be used:

- **Solution Name:** Demo.BizTalk. This is a generic solution that can hold inbound and outbound projects. You may have several projects that are common to many projects, so having everything in one solution can be very helpful. Examples of such projects would be common schemas and .NET helper classes.

- **Schemas:** There are three schemas that will be used in this solution. All three of these will be contained in a single project called Demo.BizTalk. Schemas.X850.
  ° The 850 Schema ships with BizTalk. All of the out-of-the-box schemas are contained in the `MicrosoftEdiXSDTemplates.exe` file found in `C:\Program Files (x86)\Microsoft BizTalk Server 2013\XSD_Schema\EDI`.

  ° The Target flat file schema, which represents the target data to which the 850 is being mapped. This must be created using the flat file wizard.

■ **Note** When setting a namespace, never use a numeric value alone without at least one leading text character (such as the 850 in `Demo.BizTalk. Schemas.850`), as it could result in a variety of potential naming conflicts, unexpected errors, and challenges in testing. If you wish to refer to an EDI document type directly in your namespace, use a pattern such as a leading "X", like X850.

- **Maps:** The map project will contain all maps required by the solution, and will have a namespace of Demo.BizTalk.Maps.X850.

- **Helper Library:** There will be one external .NET assembly project with the namespace of Demo.BizTalk.Helper.X850.

- **Orchestration:** There will be one orchestration used, which will be in its own project called Demo.BizTalk.Orchestrations.X850.

- **Pipeline:** There will be one custom Send pipeline project, which will be called Demo.BizTalk.Inbound.Pipelines.X850.

The Schema Project

There will be two schemas required for this project. The first is the 850 schema that ships with BizTalk. BizTalk has thousands of EDI schemas that come with it, crossing all of the document types and versions available. The second is the Target flat file that you'll be mapping the 850 to, which represents the format that the internal order processing application requires. An example of the source 850 schema is show in Figure 1-2.

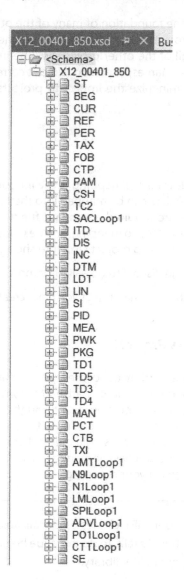

Figure1- 2. The 850 Schema

> ■ **Note** To access the EDI schemas with BizTalk, browse to the Microsoft BizTalk Server 2010 root folder and go to `XSD_Schema\EDI`. In this directory you will find a file called `MicrosoftEdiXSDTemplates.exe`. Running this file will extract all available schemas.

The schema project is the foundation of many of the other projects you will be creating, as these other projects reference them. If the schemas change during the course of development, all of the other projects will be impacted. Do everything you can to get the schemas namespaced and laid out correctly at the start of your development in order to minimize the impact to projects (especially maps) that reference these schemas.

The Map Project

The map project will allow for the mapping of the inbound 850 data into the target flat file format. The 850 data can be mapped into the target format using whatever mapping techniques are required—standard functoids, lookups, even XSLT. Chapter 4 is completely dedicated to mapping, and describes how best to approach this task. For this exercise, the map project structure should be as follows:

- Create a new project in Visual Studio called Demo.BizTalk.Maps.X850.

- Add a reference to the schema project you have created.

The .NET Helper Library Project

The .NET helper library is used by the orchestration to archive the inbound XML version of the EDI file to a database in its native XML format. This is an invaluable way of being able to access and report on data through SQL Business Intelligence (BI) platforms, such as SSRS, without having to push the 850 data to a tradition database model. The .NET class will have a single method in it that looks similar to the code shown in Listing 1-1. You can pass as many or as few parameters as you would like, depending on the needs of your reporting.

> ■ **Note** Always mark your .NET classes as Serializable, so that they can be called from anywhere within BizTalk. To do this, type [Serializable] directly above the class declaration in your helper library.

Listing 1-1. Method Called from Orchestration to Archive Data to SQL

```
public void ArchiveInboundData(string
strSourceFileName, string
strTradingPartner, XmlDocument xmlSource, string
strApprovalStatus, string strConnectionString)
{
    SqlConnection sqlConnection = new
SqlConnection(strConnectionString);
    SqlCommand sqlCommand = sqlConnection.CreateCommand();
    sqlCommand.CommandText = "spInsertInboundData";
    sqlCommand.CommandType = CommandType.StoredProcedure;
    sqlConnection.Open();

    SqlParameter sqlParameter = new SqlParameter();

    sqlParameter.ParameterName = "@vchSourceFileName";
    sqlParameter.SqlDbType = SqlDbType.VarChar;
    sqlParameter.Direction = ParameterDirection.Input;
    sqlParameter.Value = strSourceFileName;
    sqlCommand.Parameters.Add(sqlParameter);

    sqlParameter = new SqlParameter();
    sqlParameter.ParameterName = "@vchTradingPartner";
    sqlParameter.SqlDbType = SqlDbType.VarChar;
    sqlParameter.Direction = ParameterDirection.Input;
    sqlParameter.Value = strTradingPartner;
    sqlCommand.Parameters.Add(sqlParameter);

    sqlParameter = new SqlParameter();
    sqlParameter.ParameterName = "@xmlSourceData";
    sqlParameter.SqlDbType = SqlDbType.Xml;
    sqlParameter.Direction = ParameterDirection.Input;
    sqlParameter.Value = new XmlNodeReader(xmlSource);
    sqlCommand.Parameters.Add(sqlParameter);

    sqlParameter = new SqlParameter();
    sqlParameter.ParameterName = "@vchApprovalStatus";
    sqlParameter.SqlDbType = SqlDbType.VarChar;
    sqlParameter.Direction = ParameterDirection.Input;
    sqlParameter.Value = strApprovalStatus;
    sqlCommand.Parameters.Add(sqlParameter);

    sqlCommand.ExecuteNonQuery();
    sqlConnection.Close();
}
```

The stored procedure called from this method is shown in Listing 1-2. It simply takes the data passed to it and inserts it into a table. Once the data in in the table, it can be queried using standard T-SQL and XQuery.

Listing 1-2. Stored Procedure to Archive XML Data

```
CREATE PROCEDURE [spInsertInboundData]
      @vchSourceFileName As varchar(500)
      ,@vchTradingPartner As varchar(50)
      ,@xmlSourceData As xml
      ,@vchApprovalStatus As varchar(50)
AS
BEGIN

      SET NOCOUNT ON;
      INSERT tblInboundData
      (
          vchSourceFileName
          ,vchTradingPartner
          ,xmlSourceData
          ,vchApprovalStatus
          ,dtmCreateDate
      )
      VALUES
      (
          @vchSourceFileName
          ,@vchTradingPartner
          ,@xmlSourceData
          ,@vchApprovalStatus
          ,getdate()
      )
END
```

Once you have the .NET helper library built, you can reference the DLL in the orchestration project and call it to archive the inbound XML data. The next section shows how to call this referenced DLL from within an orchestration.

The Orchestration Project

In this solution, the orchestration will receive the 850 directly, map it, validate whether it can be automatically sent through or whether it must be manually reviewed, archive it to the database, and send it out in the final target format to a file directory. If archiving and the check on whether it can be automatically processed or not were not requirements, all of this could be accomplished without the use of an orchestration; the mapping could occur directly on either the receive port or send port. For this solution, however, the orchestration is used, and an example of it is shown in Figure 1-3. In order for this orchestration to work, you must add a reference to the .NET Helper DLL, the schema project, and the map project, all created earlier in this chapter.

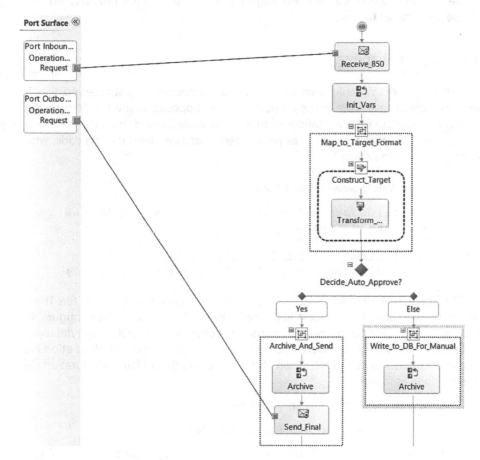

Figure1- 3. The orchestration

Details behind each of the shapes in this orchestration must be given, as several of them are Expression shapes and have important code behind them. There is no restriction as to how you populate your Expression shapes, and no requirements as to naming standards. In the case of this orchestration, all of the Expression shapes could be merged into one, but keeping them separate will allow you to see how you could add additional message types to this orchestration and be able to reuse common code.

The Receive_850 Shape

This is a simple receive shape that must be set to an orchestration message type of the 850 schema (you'll need to add a reference to this schema project from your orchestration project). Call this message msg850. The Activate property on this shape must be set to True.

The Init_Vars Shape

This shape sets variables that are specific to the document just received, which are immediately available to the orchestration (as opposed to the Init_Vars shape, which gets its data from a configuration file). The code behind this shape sets several of the fields that are passed as parameters to archive the data. The code, with notes, is shown in Listing 1-3.

Listing 1-3. Init_Vars Expression Shape Code

```
// these fields are set here so that they can be easily
written to the database
strType = "850 Inbound";
strTradingPartnerID = msg850(EDI.ISA06);
strReceivedFileName = msg850(FILE.ReceivedFileName);
```

This shape is an excellent place to read from the BizTalk configuration file. There are often variables that are best kept configurable; in this case, the configurable field is the database connection string used to connect to the SQL Server database where the data will be archived. Adding a key/value pair to your configuration file allows for rapid access and alteration of this key. Using the BizTalk configuration file can be done as follows:

- Browse to the root BizTalk Server folder.

- Open `BTSNTSvc.exe.config` in a plain text editor.

- You can add new configurable fields to the <appSettings> node of this document. An example of storing a connection string would be

    ```
    <add key="Demo.BizTalk.Archiving.ConnectionString"
    value="Data Source=BTSSQLSERVER;Initial
    Catalog=Archiving;Integrated Security=SSPI;" />
    ```

- Save the modified config file and restart the BizTalk host instance. The field can now be referenced from an Expression shape using the code shown in Listing 1-4.

Listing 1-4. Init_Vars Expression Shape Code

```
strConnectionString = System.Configuration.
ConfigurationSettings.AppSettings["Demo.BizTalk.
Archiving.ConnectionString"];
```

The Map_to_Target_Format Shape

This is the map that converts the inbound 850 into the target file format. It consists of a Construct Message shape and a Transform shape. The Transform shape references the map that was created earlier in this project.

The Decide_Auto_Approval Decision Shape

This step does the check as to whether the data can be sent straight through to the order processing system, or whether it needs to be written to a database for manual review and approval. The left-hand branch of this shape contains actions that will map it from the 850 format to the target format, archive the data, and then send the final flat file on to the final location. The right-hand branch of the shape has the steps for mapping it to the target schema and writing this XML to the database where it can be manually reviewed.

The code within the Decision shape that determines whether the data can be automatically approved or not is based on the value of BEG02 (the Purchase Order Type Code). This can be done in a variety of ways. Some fields can be promoted as distinguished fields, and accessed directly through code. Those fields that cannot be promoted (such as repeating elements or elements of certain types) can be accessed using xpath. For this demo, the decide shape's code is based on the BEG02 field being distinguished, and is `msg850.BEG.BEG02 != "AB"`. This means that anything that is not AB in the BEG02 field will allow the document to be automatically approved and sent on. Anything that has the AB value in the BEG02 fields will go down the right-hand branch of the Decision shape and will have to be manually approved. For reference, Figure 1-4 shows some of the enumerations that are available for BEG02.

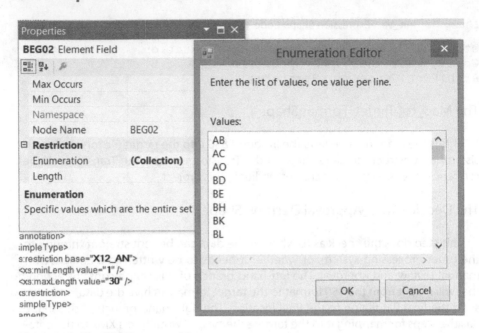

Figure1 -4. The BEG02 enumerations

The Archive Shape

This shape calls the code in the .NET library to do the actual archiving, passing in several fields as parameters. These parameters include the source file name, the trading partner, and the data to be archived. The data being archived in this case is the XML version of the 850 data, readily available to the orchestration in the inbound message. The code for archiving is shown in Listing 1-5. Notice that the inbound message (which is the orchestration message of type Demo.BizTalk. Schemas.X850 received on the Receive shape) can be converted to XML and sent straight in as a parameter.

Listing 1-5. Archive Shape Code

```
objHelper.ArchiveInboundData(strReceivedFileName,
strTradingPartnerID, (System.Xml.XmlDocument)msg850,
"Approved",strConnectionString);
```

Note that the fourth parameter is "Approved" in the left-hand block of the Decision shape, and "Needs Manual Approval" (or similar value) in the right-hand block of the Decision shape.

The Send_Final Shape

Only the left-hand block of the decision code sends an actual flat file out. This Send shape is tied to a send port, which in turn is bound to a file send or other physical port. The output is the final flat file. In the case of the right-hand block of the Decision shape, the writing of the data to the database ends the orchestration.

The Pipeline Project

The final project required is a simple custom flat file pipeline using the Flat File Assembler component that ships with BizTalk. The use of this pipeline on a send port will allow the outbound target document to be output in flat file format. The steps to create this pipeline are as follows, and the pipeline is shown in Figure 1-5.

- Create a new project called Demo.BizTalk.Inbound.Pipelines.X850.

- Add a new send pipeline to this project.

- In the pipeline GUI interface, drop a Flat File Assembler component on the Assemble stage.

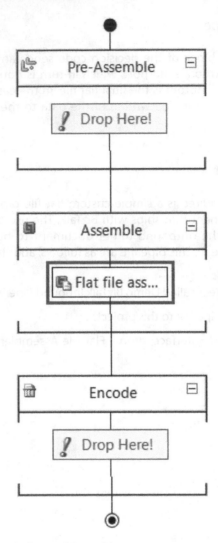

Figure1-5. The flat file pipeline and Assembler component

Setting up the BizTalk Components

With all of the Visual Studio projects completed, you will have a number of BizTalk components to deploy and configure. The first step will be to deploy the DLLs that are created when you compile your Visual Studio projects. This can be done in a variety of ways, but the one that will allow you the most control (and is the quickest) is as follows. This can be used for adding new DLLs and for updating existing DLLs. After you deploy, always restart the BizTalk host instance.

- Open BizTalk Administration Console and browse to the application where your code will be deployed. If one doesn't exist, create one called "Demo.BizTalk."

- Right-click the application and select Add and then BizTalk Assemblies.

- In the window that opens, click the Add button and add all of the assemblies for this solution: two schema DLLs, one map DLL, one orchestration DLL, and the .NET helper DLL.

- Click the Overwrite all checkbox.

- Click each DLL and make sure the first and third checkbox in the Option window is selected for each one. You must do this for every DLL that you are adding. Figure 1-6 shows the checkboxes being set (the first and third also need to be checked for the .NET assembly, though it will have several additional boxes).

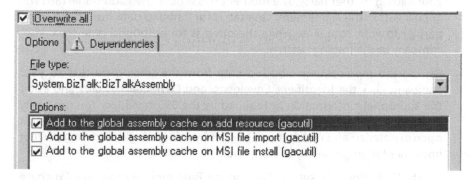

Figure1-6. The options to select when deploying assemblies

> ▓ **Note** It can be helpful to have all of your Visual Studio projects write their compiled DLLs to the same directory, as you will be deploying them to BizTalk frequently for testing. This can be done by going into the project properties for each project and setting the Output Path of the build to a common directory, like a custom folder called Binaries.

Party Settings and Agreements

The steps to configure the BizTalk Party settings that contain all of the information about how the data will be validated and what the 850 envelope settings should be are as follows:

- Create a new BizTalk Party that represents your home organization. For now, this will be called Company. All you need to set is the name.

- Create a new BizTalk Party for your trading partner; this will be named Trading Partner for this solution. You'll need to set one Party up for every trading partner you will be doing business with. Only the name needs to be set.

- Create one Agreement that represents the exchange of information between your trading partner and your company. Right-click the Company Party and create a new Agreement. Set the Protocol type to X12; the first party will automatically be set to Company, and the second party should be set to your trading partner party. The moment this is done, two additional tabs will appear within the Agreement. One tab is for inbound data from the trading partner to your company, while the other is for outbound data from your company to the trading partner.

- On the tab representing inbound data from the trading partner to your company, click the Identifiers, Envelopes, and Character set tabs and enter the appropriate information as required by the 850 envelope. You can easily access this either in a sample instance coming from the trading partner (just open in notepad and match the values) or by referencing the trading partner implementation guide (if you have one).

- On the Validation tab, set the Transaction Type property to 850 – Purchase Order.

- On the Envelopes tab, set the following values:
  - Transaction Type should be 850 – Purchase Order.
  - Version/Release should be 00401 (or 00501 if you are using the 5010 version)
  - Target namespace should be `http://schemas.microsoft.com/BizTalk/EDI/X12/2006`
  - GS1 should be PO-Purchase Order (850)
  - GS2 through GS7 should be set based on what your trading partner requires (again, see the trading partner implementation guide or a sample 850 instance from them)
  - GS8 should be 004010 (for 4010)

> ▨ **Note** The GS8 property value can be tricky to get right. If you are batching, or you have a trading partner that requires a certain value here, you may find that you have to create a custom pipeline to override this value right before it is sent to the trading partner.

The Receive Port

The inbound data will be received on an SFTP receive port. The details for configuring this port (with and without decrypted data) are given in Chapter 5. What is important to know here is that the port must not only be created, but must be bound to the orchestration. The steps for creating and binding this port are as follows:

- Create a receive port called Company.BizTalk.Receive.X850.TradingPartner. This allows for a pattern that will support multiple trading partners, if needed.

- Add a receive location to this port and call it the same thing as the receive port. Make it of type SFTP and configure the appropriate settings for the SFTP connection. Since unencrypted 850 data will be received here, set the receive pipeline to EdiReceive.

The File Send Port

The send port will be used to send the final ECSIF flat file that was mapped in the orchestration. The send port should be of type File, and should have the Send Pipeline property set to the Demo.BizTalk.Pipelines.X850.Outbound pipeline created earlier. This send port should be called Demo.BizTalk.Send.TargetData.

Orchestration Binding

The orchestration is set to pick up a file of type 850, map it to the proprietary target file, archive it, and then send out the target flat file document. Once it has been deployed, it needs to be bound to the appropriate receive and send ports. Take the following steps to bind the orchestration to the ports that were just created:

- In the BizTalk Administration Console, in the application where you are working, click the Orchestrations folder and open the Demo.BizTalk.Orchestrations. X850.Inbound orchestration you have built and deployed.

- Click the Bindings tab and set the Host property to the BizTalk Server Application host that is available.

- Set the Receive Port property to the receive port you created called Demo.
  BizTalk.Receive.X850.Receive.

- Set the Send Port property to the send port you created called Demo.BizTalk.
  Send.TargetData.

- Click OK to save these settings.

Enabling and Running the Solution

At this point, all of the components have been deployed and set up. All you need to do is enable your receive location for the inbound SFTP, start your send port for the outbound flat file, and enable your orchestration. All of this can be done through the BizTalk Administration Console. Restart the BizTalk host instance so that all of the most current settings and assemblies are loaded into memory.

Extending this Solution

There are a number of things you might want to do to make this solution more robust. The most obvious are how to handle the data that has been written to for manual approval, and improvements around determining what would cause the data to be automatically approved or not (instead of just looking at the BEG02 field). The following sections look at both improvements.

Extending this Solution with an Approval Web Site

In this demo solution, the final step of the orchestration for data that must be manually reviewed and approved is to write the data to the database with a "Needs Manual Approval" status. Now that it is in the database, something needs to be done to allow a user to view it, modify the data, and approve it. One solution is to have an ASP.NET application that shows all of the unapproved data in a grid, and loads the EDI data into human readable columns that allow for editing. The code in Listing 1-6 shows the columns of the grid being populated with data from the corresponding fields in the 850 XML, while Figure 1-7 illustrates the data grid with approval check box. This XML has been loaded directly from the database in XML format, and can be parsed for specific data.

Listing 1-6. Populating the ASP.NET Grid

```
public void InitializeDataSet(DataTableDemo dtDemo,
DataSet dsRecords, bool blnAddColumns)
{
 // Create data columns
 dtDemo.AddTextColumn("strID");
 dtDemo.AddTextColumn("vchTargetID");
 dtDemo.AddTextColumn("vchPartnerName");
 dtDemo.AddTextColumn("vchLocation");
 dtDemo.AddTextColumn("vchPONumber");
 dtDemo.AddTextColumn("vchDate");
 dtDemo.AddTextColumn("vchErrorDescription");

 dtDemo.Rows.Clear();

 // Populate rows with data
 if (dsRecords != null)
 {
  if (dsRecords.Tables.Count > 0)
  {
   foreach (DataRow row in dsRecords.Tables[0].Rows)
   {
    String strXmlDoc = row["xmlData"].ToString();

    DataRow newRow = dtDemo.AddNewRow();
    newRow["strID"] = row["uidID"].ToString();
    newRow["vchPartnerName"] = row["vchPartnerName"].
ToString();
    newRow["vchLocation"] = strGetValueFromXml(strXmlDoc,
"HAD", "Name");
    newRow["vchPONumber"] = strGetValueFromXml(strXmlDoc,
"HAD", "PONumber");
    newRow["vchTargetID"] = strGetValueFromXml(strXmlDoc,
"HAD", "TargetID");
    newRow["vchDate"] = strGetValueFromXml(strXmlDoc,
"ENV", "DateSent");
    newRow["vchErrorDescription"] =
row["vchOrigErrorDescription"].ToString();
   }
  dtDemo.AcceptChanges();
  }
 }
}
```

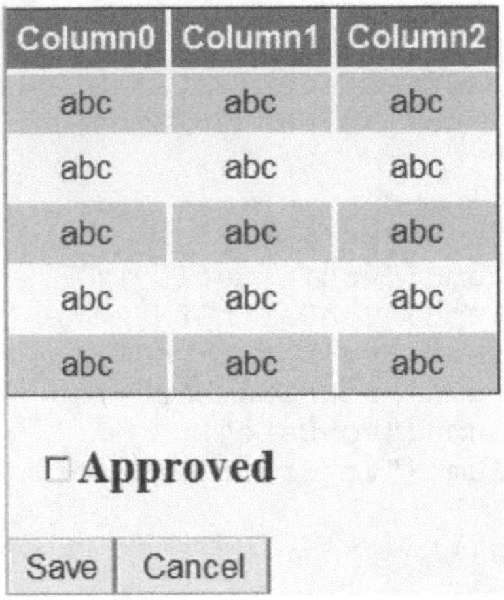

Column0	Column1	Column2
abc	abc	abc
abc	abc	abc
abc	abc	abc
abc	abc	abc
abc	abc	abc

⊓ **Approved**

Save	Cancel

Figure1 -7. Basic grid layout

While this focuses on top level fields, you should be able to envision how this could be done with repeating nodes, such as the line items. The web application can have extensive functionality that allows for editing of data and removal of line items, if required. Once the data has been fully reviewed and edited by a user, and has been marked as approved, the web application can drop a copy of the final edited 850 XML into a file drop where BizTalk can pick it up, map it to the target flat file, and deliver it to the target system—following the same path and using the same map that you created earlier for the automatic approval process in the orchestration. In this case, you would just need a receive port, receive location, and a send port (along with the map configured on either the receive or send port) in order to complete this mapping and delivery of the final data.

Extending this Solution with Better Business Rules

Currently, the only business rule that is used to determine whether the inbound 850 can be automatically approved or not happens by checking a single distinguished fields (the BEG02). Real-world scenarios will require much more robust capabilities, including checking to see if specific line items have acceptable quantities and code. For example, you may want to force manual approval when there is a quantity greater than 100 for an individual line item. You may also want to determine if the inbound location codes are valid.

In cases where you have multiple business rules that need to be reviewed, you have several options. The first is using the BizTalk Business Rules Engine (BRE). The BRE has extensive functionality and allows for any variety of rules—but it also comes with a learning curve. Frequently, in EDI environments, users have deep SQL skills and limited BizTalk skills. Building a configurable set of business rules using SQL is a compelling approach, and one that can be developed and supported fairly easily.

An example of implementing this for the location code would be the following steps:

- Get the inbound location code that you want to validate from the 850. This is found in the N104 node, and can be accessed either through xpath in the orchestration, or via a map.

- Pass the location code into a stored procedure where the lookup and validation can be done. The code in Listing 1-7 shows the C# for this call to the database. By encapsulating the call within a method in an assembly, it can be called from either within a map or within an Expression shape in an orchestration.

- Once the value has been returned, the logic in the decision shape can be based on whether it is valid or not. Any number of fields can be added into the logic of this decision shape.

Listing 1-7. Validating the Location Code

```
public int BusinessRuleLocationCodeIsValid(string
strLocationCode, string strConnectionString)
{
 SqlConnection sqlConnection = new
SqlConnection(strConnectionString);
 string strStoredProcedure =
"spBusinessRule_LocationCodeIsValid";
 SqlCommand sqlCommand = sqlConnection.CreateCommand();
 sqlCommand.CommandText = strStoredProcedure;
 sqlCommand.CommandType = CommandType.StoredProcedure;
 sqlConnection.Open();

 SqlParameter sqlParameter = new SqlParameter();
 sqlParameter = new SqlParameter();
 sqlParameter.ParameterName = "@vchLocationCode";
 sqlParameter.SqlDbType = SqlDbType.VarChar;
 sqlParameter.Direction = ParameterDirection.Input;
 sqlParameter.Value = strLocationCode;
 sqlCommand.Parameters.Add(sqlParameter);

 // value is returned
 int result = (int)sqlCommand.ExecuteScalar();
 sqlConnection.Close();

 return result;
}
```

Conclusion

You have just worked through a full implementation for receiving 850 data and mapping it to an internal proprietary flat file format. Receiving data and getting it into your system is sometimes all there is to an implementation. Other times, sending data back out to trading partners is required. The next chapter focuses on a specific implementation of sending EDI data to a trading partner, and introduces a number of topics not covered in this chapter.

The previous chapter looked at inbound 850 Purchase Order data; this chapter will look at outbound 810 Invoice data. It will introduce how to send flat file data from a receive port, map that data to an outbound 810 document, and use role links to send to a specific trading partner. You will learn how to use an adapter to pull data from an SFTP server, how to structure the source data you'll be mapping from, and how to configure role links to allow for sending to any number of trading partners dynamically from within an orchestration. The architectural overview of this solution is shown in Figure 2-1.

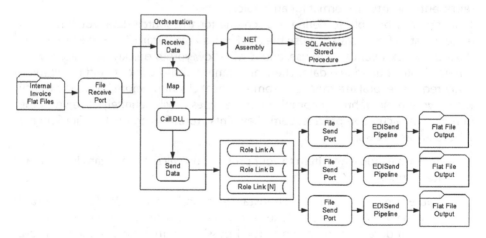

Figure2 -1. Outbound 810 solution overview

Visual Studio Solution

As discussed in the previous chapter, namespaces and project structure are essential to a successful project, so always take time in the beginning to think through all of the components that will be required and how best to name and organize them. Trying to change namespaces and project organization later in the development cycle is especially frustrating with BizTalk, given the number of components and complexity of testing. For this solution, the following Visual Studio projects and namespaces will be used:

- **Solution Name:** Demo.BizTalk. You can use the same solution you used for the project in Chapter 1.

- **Schemas:** There are two schemas that will be used in this solution, as follows. The name of this project is Demo.BizTalk.Schemas.X810.
  - ° **The 810 Schema:** This is the target schema that will be mapped to and sent out.
  - ° **The Source Schema:** This schema represents the internal representation of the invoice data.

- **Maps:** The map project will contain a single map with logic to create an 810 from the source data and will have a namespace of Demo.BizTalk.Maps.X810.

The Schema Project

There will be two schemas required for this project. The first is the 810 schema that ships with BizTalk; the second is the schema that matches the source data that represents the internal format for an invoice.

In order to be able to define the schema for the source data, you'll need to either create it from scratch or use the Flat File Schema Wizard. The Flat File Schema Wizard is an excellent tool to use, and it will allow you to quickly generate a valid schema from your source data. There are some tricks to using it, and it will most likely require several attempts and some manual cleanup before it is ready to use within your project, but for complex flat file types it will definitely save you time in the schema creation process. Some key hints around using the Flat File Schema Wizard are as follows:

- To open it, add a new item to your project. You will see the wizard listed as an item option.

- You will need a valid flat file instance to point to in order for the wizard to generate an instance. Make sure to choose a sample instance that has enough data in it to ensure that all possible formatting combinations are represented (such as columns with null values, the presence of parent and child records, etc.).

- The final output of the wizard is often two or more schemas; one will reference the other. Ideally, you will have a single schema that represents your source data, so if you have the patience to manually convert this into a single schema, you will save yourself time and frustration during the mapping process.

- If you already have a flat file schema that is similar to the format of your new source data, you should probably start by copying this and modifying it, rather than using the wizard. For example, if you have a schema that represents flat file data in a comma-delineated format with line returns separating each record, and your new source schema has pipes for the separator and a number of additional columns, then it will be quicker to modify a copy of the existing schema than to work through the wizard.

The Map Project

You will have a single map for the outbound process, which will map the source data to the target 810 structure. Details for mapping are given in Chapter 4.

The map project structure should be as follows:

- Create a new project in Visual Studio called Demo.BizTalk.Maps.X810.

- Add a reference to the schema project you have created.

The .NET Helper Library Project

You will need a C# assembly for any of the database interactions that are done from the map or from the orchestration. Generally speaking, steer clear of using the SQL adapters for communication with the database, unless you have a very specific requirement such as polling on a timed basis. The adapters add a lot of unnecessary weight to a solution, and communicating through the use of C# and an assembly keeps things simple and easy to modify and maintain. A good discussion about the .NET library can be found in Chapter 1. For the purposes of this demo, the library is used for lookups in the map (such as the one described above for the input parameter to the XSLT) and for archiving data to the database (which is outlined in full in Chapter 1). It is also used to determine the name of the party so that the orchestration can use role links to send the data.

The Orchestration Project

The process that will be taken for outbound 810s in the orchestration is shown in the following bulleted list (Figure 2-2 shows the orchestration in full). The details behind each of the shapes is also given in this section.

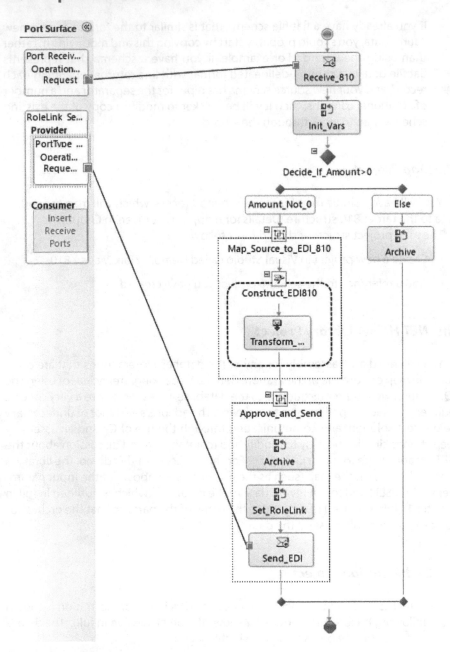

Figure2 -2. The orchestration

- The internal representation of an invoice is posted via a file drop, and the orchestration picks this up. The invoice could be for any trading partner (the identification of the trading partner that will receive the document is contained in the data itself). This data will be used at the end of the orchestration to correlate the outbound message with a specific role link and party.

- The amount of the outbound data is checked. If it is 0 (or less than 0), then it will be archived and the process will end. If it is a positive dollar amount, it will be mapped to the 810 EDI format, archived, and sent to the appropriate destination using the role link.

The Receive_810 Shape

This is the initial shape that allows the 810 to kick off the orchestration. When an 810 arrives on the port, the orchestration will be activated (set the Activate property on this shape to True). Create a message called msgSource and set the type of it to the source schema defined in your schema project.

The Init_Vars Shape

The code In this shape has a number of lookups, and sets several variables to values from the inbound file that have been promoted for use. The lookups are for fields that are used in setting the appropriate outbound party for the role link and for overriding the GS02, if necessary. The code, with notes, is shown in Listing 2-1.

Listing 2-1. Init_Vars Expression Shape Code

```
// these fields are set here so that they can be easily
written to the database
strType = "810 Outbound";
strTradingPartnerID = msgSource.ENVRecordEnvelope.ENV_
Line.CustomerID;
strReceivedFileName = msgSource(FILE.ReceivedFileName);
strPONumber = msgSource.ENVRecordEnvelope.HDR_Line.
CustomerPONumber;

intTotalInvoiceAmount =
System.Convert.ToInt32(msgSource.ENVRecordEnvelope.HDR_
Line.TotalInvAmount);

// now get the public location code - this is a simple
database lookup that
```

```
// uses a method in the helper library.
strLocationCode =
objHelper.LookupCustomerLocationCode(strTradingPartnerID,
strLocationCode);

// get the party name so that the role link can be set.
This is another
// simple lookup that uses a method in the helper assembly.
strPartyName = objHelper.LookupCustomerInfo("vchPartyName",
"ST",strLocationCode);

// get the GS02, in case it needs to be overridden.
Another lookup.
strGS02 = objHelper.LookupCustomerInfo("vchGS02",
"ST",strLocationCode);
```

Make sure to review the additional notes around how the `Init_Vars` shape can be used to read from a configuration file as outlined in Chapter 1.

The Decide_If_Amount>0 Decision Shape

This is used to illustrate how to stop the outbound flow of data, if necessary. In this case, the check is simple: `intTotalInvoiceAmount` (which was set in the Init_Vars shape) is checked, and if it is greater than 0, the left-hand branch of the decision tree will execute. If not, the right-hand branch executes, meaning the document is archived and the process ends.

The Map_Source_to_EDI_810 Shape

This references the map that was created in the mapping project earlier in this chapter. The input is `msgSource` and the output can go into a message called `msgEDI810` (and should be the 810 schema type).

The Archive Shape

This is basically the same process for archiving as was outlined in Chapter 1. The code within this shape simply takes an XML document and some additional parameters (like the document type, the party name, etc.) and passes it to a method in the helper assembly, which in turn writes the information to a SQL table.

The Set_RoleLink Shape

Since every outbound invoice is delivered to this orchestration, the orchestration has to determine who the receiving party is going to be. For example, say that there are 10 trading partners who receive invoices all on different FTP sites with different envelope information. If role links were not used, the orchestration logic would require 10 different ports just to send the data, let alone determine the envelope settings and party to associate it with. Using role links allows the orchestration to have a single outbound port, and uses the settings in the configured role links and party settings to distribute the data to the correct target party.

The code for this shape is shown here:

```
RoleLink_Send810(Microsoft.XLANGs.BaseTypes.
DestinationParty) =
new Microsoft.XLANGs.BaseTypes.Party(strPartyName,
"OrganizationName");
```

This sets the value of the destination party (which will match the name of the role link to use, configured later in the BizTalk Admin console) that will be used to send the data. In order for this to work, you will need to take the following steps to configure the role link. The role link will act and look very similar to a send port.

1. On the port surface of your orchestration, right-click and select New Role Link. In the wizard that pops up, do the following:

   a. Set the name. For this demo, it can be set to RoleLink_Send810.

   b. Create a new Role Link Type. The name can be PortType_Send_EDI810

   c. Set the role link to "Provider."

   d. Create a port type within the Provider role link that is set to the Send_ EDI810 port type, has one-way communication and public access.

2. Create a new Role Link Type in the orchestration view of your orchestration, and link it to the role link "port" you created in the previous step.

The Send_EDI Shape

This shape needs to be set to the outbound message created from the map (the 810 EDI) and connected to the Provider type on the role link. The type of the message should match the outbound port type within the Provider role link.

The Pipeline Project

The final project required is a simple custom flat file pipeline using the Flat File Disassembler component that ships with BizTalk. The use of this pipeline on a receive port will allow the inbound source document to be converted from the flat file format into XML. Figure 2-3 shows this pipeline. The steps to create this pipeline are as follows:

- Create a new project called Demo.BizTalk.Outbound.Pipelines.X810.

- Add a new receive pipeline to this project.

- In the pipeline GUI interface, drop a Flat File Disassembler component on the Disassemble stage.

- In the properties of the disassembler component, set the Document Schema property to the Demo.BizTalk.Schemas.X810 schema created earlier in this project (you may have to deploy the schema DLL in order to have access to this).

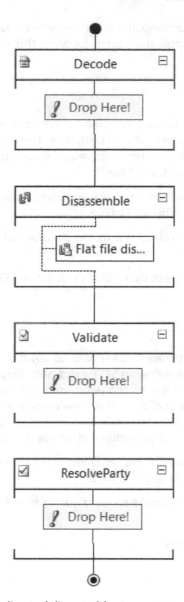

Figure2- 3. The flat file pipeline and disassembler component

Setting up the BizTalk Components

For this solution, you will need to set up the receive port and receive location, bind the orchestration, and configure the role link settings.

Before configuring these components, you will want to deploy your Visual Studio assemblies to the BizTalk application. Steps for doing this are outlined in Chapter 1.

File Receive Port

The input to this solution is a simple file receive port. A flat file will arrive on a file drop and will be picked up by the orchestration. This receive location associated with this port needs to have the pipeline created earlier in this chapter associated with it, so that it can process the flat file.

- Create a new receive port and receive location combination, both named Demo.BizTalk.Receive.Invoice.FlatFile.

- Set the Type to File and point it to the directory where the flat files will be dropped.

- Set the receive pipeline to Demo.BizTalk.Outbound.Pipelines.X810.

SFTP Send Ports

Each trading partner can receive their data via any protocol they require. In this case, you will look at configuring an SFTP send port. This port will be associated with the BizTalk party, and will be triggered from the orchestration through the role link that you will soon configure. There will be one send port created for each trading partner. In order to illustrate role links, two trading partners will be set up, so two send ports will need to be configured for this demo.

- Create two new send ports named Demo.BizTalk.Send.TradingPartner_A and Demo.BizTalk.Send.TradingPartner_B.

- Set the Type to SFTP. Details for configuring the SFTP adapter are given in Chapter 5.

- Set the send pipeline to EdiSend.

> ■ **Note** A single send port can be used to send numerous EDI transaction types. You are configuring these for the 810, but if you were to deliver more transaction types (such as an 855, for example) you would not need to configure a new port, unless the actual physical location that is being delivered to is different for the various document types.

Party Settings

In the previous chapter, you looked at configuring the base settings for the BizTalk Party and Agreement on inbound data. You can reuse these settings, or you can configure fresh trading partners. The home organization can remain the same. The basics of what you will want are as follows (Figure 2-4 shows a high-level summary of parties and agreements):

- Three trading partners, one representing the home organization (your company), and one for each of the recipient organizations that the 810 EDI documents are being sent to.

- Two agreements, one for each recipient organization.

- In the agreements, the critical information to configure is as follows:
  - The Identifiers tab must be set up on both the inbound and outbound settings.
  - The Send Port tab on the outbound settings (Home Company ➤ Trading Partner) must have a reference to the SFTP send port configured earlier in this chapter. Make sure that the send port you are setting up corresponds to the correct party.
  - The Envelope tab must have the information for the 810 transaction type configured.
    - Transaction Type should be 810-Invoice
    - Version is set to 00401 (match your correct version)
    - Target namespace should be `http://schemas.microsoft.com/BizTalk/EDI/X12/2006`
    - GS1 should be IN-Invoice Information (810)
    - GS2 through GS7 should be set based on what your trading partner requires (see the trading partner implementation guide or a sample 810 instance from them)
    - GS8 should be 004010 (or 005010 for 5010, you will need to match the right version)

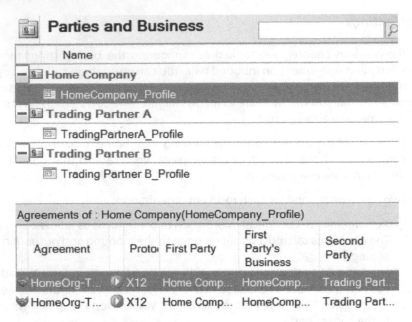

Figure2-4. Parties and agreements

> **Note** The role links work in conjunction with the parties, and whatever send port is associated with the party in the agreements (and corresponds to the type of data being sent) will be used to send the physical file.

Configuring the Role Links

The final step for this solution is the setup and configuration of the role links. The orchestration is set to pick up invoices that could be delivered to any trading partner in the 810 format. For the purposes of this demo, two trading partners have been configured, but in real-world scenarios you may be required to set up dozens of trading partners, all receiving the 810 transaction type. For each trading partner, you will need to do the following:

- Configure a BizTalk party and create a new agreement (this is where the envelope and other information unique to a trading partner is configured).

- Set up a send port. A send port can be used to send multiple EDI document types (810, 855, etc.), but each trading partner will need to have its own dedicated send port.

- Set up a role link. This enables the orchestration to dynamically send to the appropriate target party.

To set up a role link, take these steps:

- Open the BizTalk Admin console and click the Role Links in the Demo.BizTalk application.

- In the right-hand pane, double-click the Provider option (this represents parties that will be sent to).

- Click the Enlist button. In the window that opens, select the trading partner that you will be configuring a role link for; you will enlist one role link for each of the trading partners receiving an 810 document. Click OK to save these. Figure 2-5 shows the settings in this window.

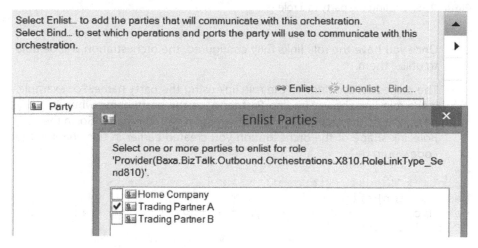

Figure2- 5. Enlisting a party for role link configuration

- Back in the main window, double-click each party to bind them.

- In the window that opens for binding, select the send port to associate with the orchestration's port operation. This send port should be unique to the trading partner (although it can be used for multiple document types). Figure 2-6 shows this binding for a trading partner.

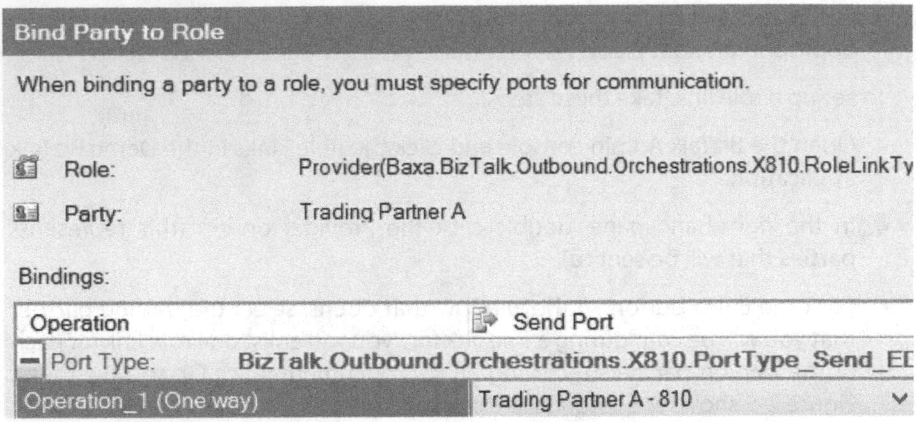

Bind Party to Role

When binding a party to a role, you must specify ports for communication.

Role: Provider(Baxa.BizTalk.Outbound.Orchestrations.X810.RoleLinkTy

Party: Trading Partner A

Bindings:

Operation		⇨ Send Port
─ Port Type:	BizTalk.Outbound.Orchestrations.X810.PortType_Send_EL	
Operation_1 (One way)		Trading Partner A - 810 ∨

Figure2 -6. Binding the party to a role

- Once you have the role links fully configured, the orchestration will be able to utilize them.

- The orchestration binds to the role link using the party name. For example, if the role link shows "Trading Partner A" as the party name when it is has been bound, the orchestration must refer to it with this name. So, in the Set_RoleLink shape of the orchestration you created earlier in this chapter, the code would be

```
RoleLink_Send810(Microsoft.XLANGs.BaseTypes.
DestinationParty) =
new Microsoft.XLANGs.BaseTypes.Party("Trading Partner A",
"OrganizationName");
```

Enabling and Running the Solution

In order for this solution to work, the receive location must be enabled, the send ports must be started, and the orchestration must be running. You will want to restart the BizTalk host instance to ensure that all of the most recent configurations and components are loaded into memory.

Conclusion

This chapter covered some critical aspects of developing BizTalk EDI solutions within the manufacturing and shipping space. You will likely find that the requirements for your specific implementation vary from the specific pattern outlined in this solution, but you should have more than enough information now to be able to architect an efficient and highly maintainable outbound solution. The next chapter will look at an implementation that does not require an orchestration, so that you can see how a simple implementation differs from the more involved ones covered so far in this book.

Chapter 3

Solution: Sending845Da ta

The first two chapters outlined solutions that had a number of components and steps. You will now look at a solution that uses only schemas, ports, maps, and party configurations. The architectural overview of this solution is shown in Figure 3-1.

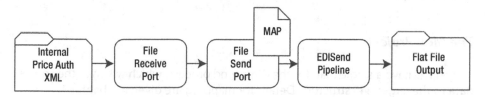

Figure3- 1. Outbound 845 solution overview

> ■ **Note** This chapter builds on foundational concepts outlined in the first two chapters, and assumes knowledge of best practices that have also already been outlined.

Visual Studio Solution

For this solution, the following Visual Studio projects and namespaces will be used:

- **Solution Name:** Demo.BizTalk. You can use the same solution you used for the project in the earlier chapters, or you can create a new one.

- **Schemas:** There are two schemas that will be used in this solution, as follows. The name of this project is Demo.BizTalk.Schemas.X845.

- ° **The 845 Schema:** This is the target schema that will be mapped to and sent out.
- ° **The Source Schema:** This schema represents the internal representation of the price authorization data.

- **Maps:** The map project will contain a single map with logic to create an 845 from the source data, and will have a namespace of Demo.BizTalk. Maps.X845.

The Schema Project

Two schemas are required for this project. The first is the 845 schema that ships with BizTalk, the second is the schema representing the internal format of the price authorization data. For this solution, it will be an XML document dropped on a file drop.

The Map Project

You will have a single map for the outbound process, which will map the source data to the target 845 structure. Details for mapping are given in Chapter 4.

The map project structure should be as follows:

- Create a new project in Visual Studio called Demo.BizTalk.Maps.X845.

- Add a reference to the schema project you have created.

Setting up the BizTalk Components

For this solution, you will need to set up the receive port and receive location, and configure a send port to subscribe to this receive port.

Before configuring these components, you will want to deploy your Visual Studio assemblies to the BizTalk application. Steps for doing this are outlined in Chapter 1.

File Receive Port

The input to this solution is a simple file receive port. An XML document will be picked up by this port.

- Create a new receive port and receive location combination, both named Demo.BizTalk.Receive.PriceAuthorization.XML.

- Set the type to File, and point it to the directory where the XML will be dropped.

- Set the receive pipeline to the default XMLReceive.

File Send Port

This port, which will be associated with a BizTalk party shortly, will subscribe to all data arriving on the receive port you just configured, and will map and deliver the data. Take the following steps:

- Create one send port named Demo.BizTalk.Send.X845.

- Set the type to File.

- Set the send pipeline to EdiSend.

- On the Filters tab, set the filter to BTS.ReceivePortName == [*the name of the receive port you just configured, which is Demo.BizTalk.Receive. PriceAuthorization.XML*].

- On the Outbound Maps tab, select the map that you just deployed (Demo. BizTalk.Maps.X845).

Note You can add multiple maps to a send port, which will allow you to reuse it to send a variety of outbound document types. When you have multiple maps, BizTalk will iterate through each of them to see if the document that the send port just received matches any of the source document schemas in the maps. It will use the first map it finds that matches this source schema.

Party Settings

You can reuse most of the party settings that you have created in previous chapters. The required components are as follows:

- Two trading partners, one representing the home organization (your company), and one for the recipient organization that the 845 EDI documents are being sent to.

- One agreement (again, if you have configured an agreement from an earlier solution in this book, you can reuse it; just extend it to handle the 845).

- In the agreement, the key information to configure is as follows:
  - ° The Identifiers tab must be set up on both the inbound and outbound settings.
  - ° The Send Port tab on the outbound settings (Home Company ➤ Trading Partner) must have a reference to the send port configured earlier in this chapter.
  - ° The Envelope tab must have the information for the 845 transaction type configured.
    - Transaction Type should be 845-Price Authorization Acknowledgement/Status
    - Version is set to 00401 or 00501 (match your correct version)
    - Target namespace should be http://schemas.microsoft.com/BizTalk/EDI/X12/2006
    - GS1 should be PA-Price Authorization Acknowledgement/Status (845)
    - GS2 through GS7 should be set based on what your trading partner requires (see the Trading Partner Implementation Guide or a sample 845 instance from them)
    - GS8 should be 004010 (or 005010 for 5010, you will need to match the right version)

Enabling and Running the Solution

In order for this solution to work, the receive location and the send port must be enabled. You will want to restart the BizTalk host instance to ensure that all of the most recent configurations and components are loaded into memory.

Conclusion

You have just configured and deployed the simplest of EDI solutions. It is important to understand the core components required in an implementation. When building a solution, always think of the simplest process, and then build in the additional architectural components required by your specific implementation. You have now looked at two complex solutions (requiring multiple BizTalk components) and one simple solution. The next chapter outlines how to succeed with mapping, and covers a number of mapping solutions.

Constructing and deconstructing the data in the various EDI formats available is a task that requires both analysis and development skills. Most of the document types within the manufacturing and shipping space are fairly straightforward to handle, but you will run across node structures and mapping requirements that will pose challenges.

It is possible to look at an implementation guide and make intelligent decisions about how data should be mapped. To improve your chances for a compliant EDI document early in the development process, make sure to take the following steps:

- Whenever possible, get access to an actual EDI document that is being used for the specific trading partner you are working with. Implementation guides are good for reference, but as a developer, having access to the actual file is of immense value. It allows for side-by-side comparisons between what you are creating in BizTalk and what you know is a valid format.

- There are many alternative ways to populate data in the various formats, and it is common to have mapping requirements that are unique to a trading partner. Be prepared to have maps that are very different between partners, whether inbound or outbound.

■ **Note** Don't try to create a single map that will work for all of your trading partners—this requires too much logic in a map. One map per partner per document type is the general rule for mapping.

- In some cases, mapping is best done in multiple stages. It is always nice to be able to map a source document to the target EDI document (or vice versa) in a single map, but it does not always allow for the easiest or most maintainable solution. When developing your maps, think about the next person who may have to take these maps over from you at a later time. Will they be able to interpret what you have done and make modifications to it, if needed?

When planning your mapping, think about ways to simplify your logic, and determine if creating several maps that take the data through several phases of transformation could ease your development.

- The topics in this chapter will cover how to approach mapping various EDI formats with several development techniques. It won't be possible to demonstrate how to map a document in its entirety, but with some key foundational information available and some patience, you will be able to create maps that are well architected and use the most appropriate mapping technologies.

> ■ **Note** When building outbound maps where you have control over the source data you are mapping from, try to pre-format as much data as possible so that once it gets to the BizTalk map, there is as little additional mapping needed as possible. The less complex your map is, the easier your solution will be to develop, test, and maintain.

BizTalkM apping Technologies

There are several technologies that you will need to be very comfortable with in order to have the tools available in BizTalk to handle the mapping that is associated with working the various document implementations. The BizTalk Visual Studio map is the canvas for development, but there are numerous options for mapping the data. These mapping technologies are as follows:

- **Functoids:** There are many functoids available to you, and it is possible to implement almost all mapping requirements without the use of externals scripts. However, trying to implement all of your maps without the use of external scripts is a mistake, and will most likely lead to complex and unmaintainable maps.

- **Inline .NET Code:** The Scripting functoid in the mapper allows for a variety of script languages. You can accomplish quite a bit within these scripts, but you have limited access to libraries. Only those libraries available to XLANG can be used within a .NET Scripting functoid.

- **External .NET Assemblies:** When you need the power of the full .NET engine and associated libraries, you'll want to develop an actual assembly with methods that can be called from the map. Some tasks, such as interactions with a database, are often best done in external assemblies.

- **Inline XSLT:** This is a very important skill to develop, and should not be overlooked or avoided. Tasks that could take many functoids or complex external .NET scripts can be done quickly using XSLT. Some mapping issues in more complex documents can't even be solved without the use of XSLT. While there will be some ramp-up in learning this scripting language, it will be worth your investment.

- **External XSLT:** In most cases, you will use the functoids and mapping options available in the map to complete your solution. In other cases, you may want to simply shell out to an external XSLT file to handle the mapping.

- **SQL Stored Procedures:** When dealing with business rules, data level transformations, or lookups, you may want to create stored procedures and deal with logic there. Calling a stored procedure through an external .NET assembly from a map is an easy architecture to build, and can be of great benefit. Several examples of calling a DLL from an orchestration were given in earlier chapters, and this approach can be applied to calls within maps.

When determining how to map and what technology or technologies to use, take the following steps to ensure you are making the right decision:

- Plan your architecture; wait to start development. It is easy and tempting to just start mapping. In fact, 80% of the mapping you'll do is straightforward, and you'll find that you make quick progress with much of the implementation. Then, as you begin on the final 20%, you'll start to run into hurdles that are very difficult to overcome, especially if you haven't built the rest of your map to support this 20%. You'll find that loops you've built and nodes you've mapped have to be rewritten to support your requirements. So, in short, plan your mapping before you start development.

- Start with the most complex nodes first. Assess what is the most complicated aspect of mapping, and deal with that first. It will ensure that you are developing with the right approach, and if you find that you have to rethink your approach, you haven't wasted a lot of time on other mappings.

- Use XSLT. There are so many complexities in mapping that are reduced and simplified by using XSLT that it is a mistake not to plan on using it extensively in your maps.

Looking at actual examples of mapping technologies is the topic of the next section. With these specific examples in front of you, you should be able to jump into the development of your maps with a solid direction as to how to implement.

Using Inline C# to Map ITD04 and Other Dates

One item that you will likely have to deal with in the creation of the 810 is the format of certain date fields, such as the ITD04. Your inbound data format will likely differ from the requirements of the format for these fields, and some conversion will likely need to take place. Converting dates can be done in a variety of ways, including a pattern of multiple standard functoids (string concatenates, rights, lefts, finds, etc.). In this case, you will look at some inline C#, as shown in Listing 4-1. This assumes that the date format is YYYYMMDD and that there is a parameter (period) indicating how many days need to be added to this date.

Listing 4-1. Date Conversion Using Inline C#

```
public string getDateInfo(string date, int period)
{
// convert to valid date format
 string newDate = date.Substring(4,2) + "/" +
date.Substring(6,2) + "/" + date.Substring(0,4);

 DateTime dt = DateTime.Parse(newDate);

// add the period and convert it to new date format
 newDate = dt.AddDays(period).ToString("yyyyMMdd");

 return newDate;
}
```

> ■ **Note** Inline functions can be used multiple times in a map by creating a script functoid that has no inputs or outputs and placing within it the function (or functions) that you want accessible globally to the map.

Date Conversions Using an External .NET Assembly

In some cases, you may have requirements that are either very involved, or need to be used across multiple maps and/or orchestrations. Building on the date conversion from the inline sample, imagine a scenario where the source data was generated by SQL Server and all dates are in the format similar to 2012-10-21T04:00:20.043. The target date fields (such as ITD04) need to have this format converted to 20121021. This formatting must be applied to many fields, and the code used to convert from the SQL format to the EDI format needs to be used each time.

There are many options for implementation, including using standard functoids, but the most appropriate solution that uses the least amount of components is an external .NET assembly. If standard functoids were used, you would have to use several string functoids in a pattern, and this pattern would have to be applied over and over in the map. With the inline C# option, you would have to paste the same code into multiple maps. With the external .NET assembly, the code is written once, and a Scripting functoid is dropped wherever the conversion needs to take place.

If the conversion logic needs to be changed for whatever reason (such as the source data format changes), then it only has to be changed in one place (the referenced DLL) and not everywhere the conversion is taking place (which would be the case with the functoid pattern).

In order to build this using an external .NET assembly, take the steps in the following exercise.

MAPPING WITH AN EXTERNAL .NET ASSEMBLY

This exercise will walk through calling an external assembly to format dates in EDI-compliant formats.

1. Create a .NET class library. Give it a namespace of Maps.Helper, and a class name of Helper.

2. Create a method called FormatDate, which has one input parameter in string format. Write the code to convert from the source format to the target EDI format. An example of this code is shown in Listing 4-2.

3. Compile the assembly and reference it in your Visual Studio map project.

4. In the map, drop a Scripting functoid on the map surface. Drag the input from the source document's date field, and drop it on the target document's date field.

5. Open the Scripting functoid and click the Script Functoid Configuration tab. Set the script type to External Assembly, then select your Script assembly, class, and method from the drop-downs. If you assembly is not shown, try closing Visual Studio and reopening. In some cases, you may have to install the DLL to the Global Assembly Cache (GAC; see next step) in order to be able to see it.

6. Test the map. This requires that the assembly be deployed to the GAC. Chapter 1 discusses how to deploy assemblies via the BizTalk Administration Console, which places them in the GAC.

An example of this functoid being used on the ITD04 field is shown in Figure 4-1.

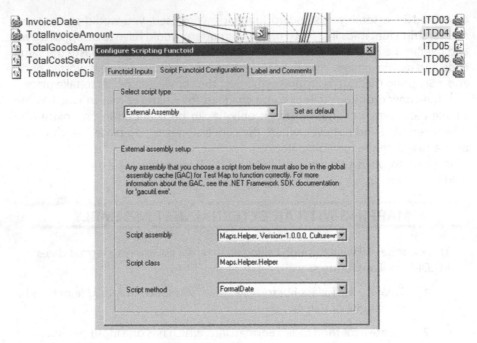

Figure4 -1. Calling an external assembly from a map

Listing 4-2. Formatting a Date

```
public string FormatDate(string dateString)
{
 if (string.IsNullOrEmpty(dateString) == false)
 {
  try
  {
   DateTime date = XmlConvert.ToDateTime(dateString,
    XmlDateTimeSerializationMode.Local);
   return date.ToString("yyyyMMdd");
  }
  catch
  {
   return string.Empty;
  }
 }
 else
 {
  return string.Empty;
 }
}
```

Mapping the N1Loop1 with Inline XSLT Call Template

Another item you will have to deal with in mapping the 810 is the creation of the N1Loop1, a repeating node that likely won't map directly to your source data. This is a case where using inline XSLT will be of use and will eliminate the complexity of trying to deal with this through the use of standard functoids. Figure 4-2 shows the map pattern for this. On the left is the source data, and there is one field, EDIReferenceCode, being used as an input parameter to the inline XSLT Call Template script (the functoid on the right). This first parameter represents the N103 field. The script functoid on the left is another input to the inline XSLT, and is a database lookup for the N104 field.

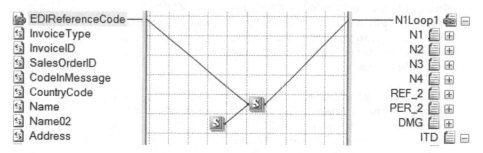

Figure4- 2. Using inline XSLT call template to map the N1Loop1

As you know, the N1Loop1 can consist of many addresses. Some are static (like the source RI company data) while others are dynamic (based on the source data). The example XSLT script in Listing 4-3 shows how to deal with both static and dynamic data, along with handling two input parameters to the script.

Listing 4-3. Inline XSLT Call Template for the N1Loop1

```
<xsl:template name="N1Loop">
<xsl:param name="N103" />
<xsl:param name="N104" />

<xsl:element name="N1Loop1">
 <!-- hard coded Source Company values -->
 <xsl:element name="N1">
  <xsl:element name="N101">RI</xsl:element>
  <xsl:element name="N102">Demo Company</xsl:element>
  <xsl:element name="N103">91</xsl:element>
  <xsl:element name="N104">123456789</xsl:element>
 </xsl:element>
 <xsl:element name="N3">
  <xsl:element name="N301">Department 123</xsl:element>
```

```xml
    </xsl:element>
  <xsl:element name="N4">
   <xsl:element name="N401">Grand Junction</xsl:element>
   <xsl:element name="N402">CO</xsl:element>
   <xsl:element name="N403">81502</xsl:element>
  </xsl:element>
</xsl:element>

<!-- loop through dynamic number of source segments for
remaining -->
<xsl:for-each select="//HAD_Lines">
 <xsl:element name="N1Loop1">
  <xsl:element name="N1">
   <xsl:if test="CodeInMessage = 'INV'">
    <xsl:element name="N101">BT</xsl:element>
    <xsl:element name="N102">
     <xsl:value-of select="Name" />
    </xsl:element>
   </xsl:if>
   <xsl:if test="CodeInMessage = 'DEL'">
    <xsl:element name="N101">ST</xsl:element>
    <xsl:element name="N102">
     <xsl:value-of select="Name" />
    </xsl:element>
    <xsl:element name="N103"><xsl:value-of select ="$N103"/>
</xsl:element>
    <xsl:element name="N104"><xsl:value-of select ="$N104"/>
</xsl:element>
   </xsl:if>
  </xsl:element>
  <xsl:if test="Name02 != ''">
  <xsl:element name="N2">
   <xsl:element name="N201">
    <xsl:value-of select="Name02" />
   </xsl:element>
  </xsl:element>
  </xsl:if>
  <xsl:element name="N3">
   <xsl:element name="N301">
    <xsl:value-of select="Address" />
   </xsl:element>
  </xsl:element>
  <xsl:element name="N4">
   <xsl:element name="N401">
    <xsl:value-of select="translate(substring-before
(City,','),' ','')"/>
   </xsl:element>
```

```
  <xsl:element name="N402">
   <xsl:value-of select="translate(substring-after
(City,',')),' ',''')"/>
   </xsl:element>
   <xsl:element name="N403">
    <xsl:value-of select="ZipCode"/>
   </xsl:element>
  </xsl:element>
 </xsl:element>
</xsl:for-each>
</xsl:template>
```

Inline XSLT is amazingly useful with BizTalk mapping. It gives the level of control over parsing and manipulating data that is essential. The ability to look throughout the source data, regardless of where data lies in the overall hierarchy and node structure, allows for building the logic that may be required without having to build complex functoid pattern solutions.

Using Standard Functoids to Map the CTT Segment

On occasion, using standard functoids can be unpredictably simple. In the case of mapping the CTT node (Transaction Totals) on the 810, for example, getting the total number of line items and total quantity delivered can be done using a Record Count functoid and a Cumulative Sum functoid, as show in Figure 4-3.

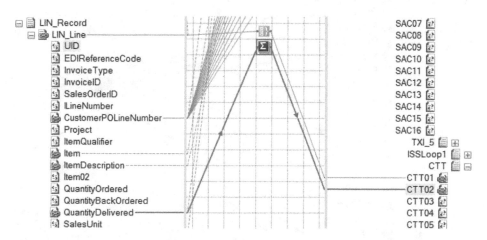

Figure4- 3. Mapping the CTT01 and CTT02 totals

For situations where you are mapping all of the line items to the output, these two functoids are extremely helpful and the map is simple. However, if you were required to filter out some of the outbound line items, and provide a total in CTT01 and CTT02 only for those lines that were mapped, you'll run into a situation where once again you'll want to use inline XSLT, as the options for mapping via standard functoids are not good.

Case Statements and the PO1Loop1 Node

When mapping the inbound 850, you'll likely run into some interesting conditions when dealing with the PO1Loop1 data. Trading Partners can use any combination of the PO106 – PO125 data to represent their item data. You may find that in order to map to your inbound schema, you'll need to determine what data is stored in which PO segment, and will have to map this in some particular order. One way of doing this is through inline C# that does the filtering and provides an output for other functoids in the map (such as a Value Mapping functoid). Figure 4-4 shows looping on the PO1Loop1 node, and each of the PO106 – PO125 nodes going to a single Scripting functoid. The C# for this functoid is shown in Listing 4-4.

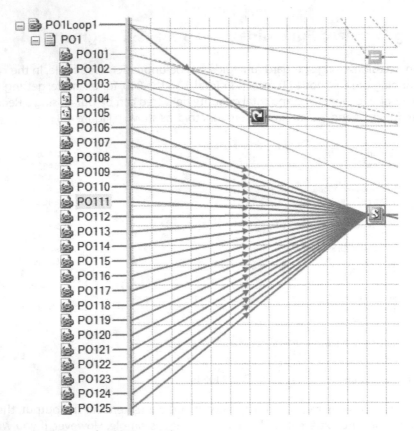

Figure4 -4. Mapping the PO1Loop1 data

Listing 4-4. Filtering the PO Data in Inline C#

```
// must find VC element if present. If not, return PO107
(the first)
public string FindCorrectItem(string PO106, string PO107,
string PO108, string PO109, string PO110, string PO111,
string PO112, string PO113, string PO114, string PO115,
string PO116, string PO117, string PO118, string PO119,
string PO120, string PO121, string PO122, string PO123,
string PO124, string PO125)
{
 if(PO108 == "VC")
  return PO109;
 if(PO110 == "VC")
  return PO111;
 if(PO112 == "VC")
  return PO113;
 if(PO114 == "VC")
  return PO115;
 if(PO116 == "VC")
  return PO117;
 if(PO118 == "VC")
  return PO119;
 if(PO120 == "VC")
  return PO121;
 if(PO122 == "VC")
  return PO123;
 if(PO124 == "VC")
  return PO125;
 else
  return PO107;
}
```

Mapping the PADLoop1 Nodes

The final example we'll look at is the detailed mapping of the outbound 845's PADLoop1 nodes. There are a number of nodes that are challenging to construct, especially depending on the structure of the source document. The map in Figure 4-5 shows all of the functoids that are used for mapping the various nodes. There are straight mappings: one loop, one iteration, and several XSLT functoids. Each of the elements mapped are described in the following sections.

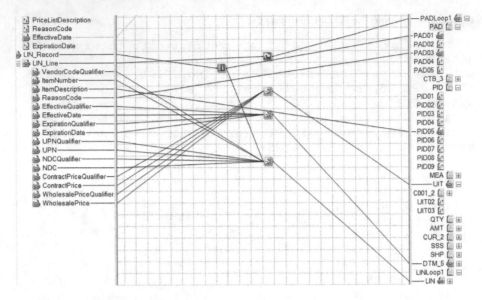

Figure4 -5. The PADLoop1 mapping

The PADLoop1

This is the containing element and has an inbound Looping functoid attached to it. This will force a new loop instance of the PAD segments for each line item in the source data.

The PAD Elements

There is simple mapping in place for the PAD01 and PAD03 elements. PAD01 is the output of the Iteration functoid, which gives a simple line count. PAD03 shows a straight mapping from the reason code in the source data.

The PID Segment

More simple mappings here, but what is not shown in the map from Figure 4-5 is that the value of PID01 and others are given default values in the properties on the target elements. For example, PID01 is defaulted to "F", as shown in Figure 4-6. This can be done by setting the Value property of the PID01 element in the properties dialogue box.

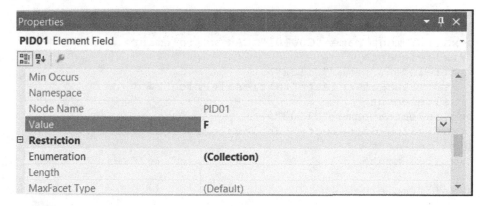

Figure4- 6. Setting a default value on PID01

> ■ **Note** While setting default values in the Value property is an option, you won't have visibility on the map that the field has been mapped. If you want to keep visibility, place the default value in a simple Concatenate functoid and use this as the input to your target field.

The UIT Segment

The UIT data contains pricing and other information. For this mapping, a Scripting functoid with an inline XSLT call template is used. Four parameters are passed as inputs. The code is shown in Listing 4-5.

Listing 4-5. XSLT for the UIT Segment

```
<xsl:template name="UIT">
<xsl:param name="ContractPriceQualifier" />
<xsl:param name="ContractPrice" />
<xsl:param name="WholesalePriceQualifier" />
<xsl:param name="WholesalePrice" />

<xsl:element name="ns0:UIT">
<xsl:element name="ns0:C001_2">
 <xsl:element name="C00101">CA</xsl:element>
</xsl:element>
<xsl:element name="UIT02">
 <xsl:value-of select="$ContractPrice"/>
</xsl:element>
<xsl:element name="UIT03">
 <xsl:value-of select="$ContractPriceQualifier"/>
</xsl:element>
</xsl:element>
```

```
<xsl:element name="ns0:UIT">
<xsl:element name="ns0:C001_2">
 <xsl:element name="C00101">CA</xsl:element>
</xsl:element>
<xsl:element name="UIT02">
 <xsl:value-of select="$WholesalePrice"/>
</xsl:element>
<xsl:element name="UIT03">
 <xsl:value-of select="$WholesalePriceQualifier"/>
</xsl:element>
</xsl:element>

</xsl:template>
```

The DTM_5 Segment

The date and time information stored in this segment shows another instance of mapping using XSLT. The XSLT call template code is shown in Listing 4-6.

Listing 4-6. XSLT for the DTM Segment

```
<xsl:template name="DTM_5">
<xsl:param name="EffectiveQualifier" />
<xsl:param name="EffectiveDate" />
<xsl:param name="ExpirationQualifier" />
<xsl:param name="ExpirationDate" />

<xsl:element name="ns0:DTM_5">
 <xsl:element name="DTM01">
  <xsl:value-of select="$EffectiveQualifier"/>
 </xsl:element>
 <xsl:element name="DTM02">
  <xsl:value-of select="$EffectiveDate"/>
 </xsl:element>
</xsl:element>

<xsl:element name="ns0:DTM_5">
 <xsl:element name="DTM01">
  <xsl:value-of select="$ExpirationQualifier"/>
 </xsl:element>
 <xsl:element name="DTM02">
  <xsl:value-of select="$ExpirationDate"/>
 </xsl:element>
</xsl:element>

</xsl:template>
```

The LIN Segment

All of the line item information is handled in the XSLT call template code shown in Listing 4-7. It introduces some `if` statements into the logic.

Listing 4-7. XSLT for the LIN Segment

```
<xsl:template name="LIN">
<xsl:param name="LineNumber" />
<xsl:param name="UPNQualifier" />
<xsl:param name="UPN" />
<xsl:param name="NDCQualifier" />
<xsl:param name="NDC" />
<xsl:param name="VendorQualifier" />
<xsl:param name="ItemNumber" />

<xsl:element name="ns0:LIN">
 <xsl:element name="LIN01">
  <xsl:value-of select="$LineNumber"/>
 </xsl:element>

 <xsl:if test="$UPNQualifier != ''">
  <xsl:element name="LIN02">
   <xsl:value-of select="$UPNQualifier"/>
  </xsl:element>
  <xsl:element name="LIN03">
   <xsl:value-of select="$UPN"/>
  </xsl:element>
 </xsl:if>

 <xsl:if test="$UPNQualifier != '' and $NDCQualifier = ''">
  <xsl:element name="LIN04">
   <xsl:value-of select="$VendorQualifier"/>
  </xsl:element>
  <xsl:element name="LIN05">
   <xsl:value-of select="$ItemNumber"/>
  </xsl:element>
 </xsl:if>

 <xsl:if test="$UPNQualifier = '' and $NDCQualifier != ''">
  <xsl:element name="LIN02">
   <xsl:value-of select="$NDCQualifier"/>
  </xsl:element>
  <xsl:element name="LIN03">
   <xsl:value-of select="$NDC"/>
  </xsl:element>
```

```
  <xsl:element name="LIN04">
   <xsl:value-of select="$VendorQualifier"/>
  </xsl:element>
  <xsl:element name="LIN05">
   <xsl:value-of select="$ItemNumber"/>
  </xsl:element>
 </xsl:if>

 <xsl:if test="$UPNQualifier = '' and $NDCQualifier = ''">
  <xsl:element name="LIN02">
   <xsl:value-of select="$VendorQualifier"/>
  </xsl:element>
  <xsl:element name="LIN03">
   <xsl:value-of select="$ItemNumber"/>
  </xsl:element>
 </xsl:if>

 <xsl:if test="$UPNQualifier != '' and $NDCQualifier != ''">
  <xsl:element name="LIN04">
   <xsl:value-of select="$NDCQualifier"/>
  </xsl:element>
  <xsl:element name="LIN05">
   <xsl:value-of select="$NDC"/>
  </xsl:element>
  <xsl:element name="LIN06">
   <xsl:value-of select="$VendorQualifier"/>
  </xsl:element>
  <xsl:element name="LIN07">
   <xsl:value-of select="$ItemNumber"/>
  </xsl:element>
 </xsl:if>
</xsl:element>
</xsl:template>
```

Conclusion

This chapter gave an overview of how to be successful with your mapping solutions. It also gave specific examples around mapping several elements, and provided direction on how to implement inline scripts for complex maps. With the proper use of the techniques outlined in this chapter, and especially through the use of XSLT, you will be able to solve any mapping problem that may arise.

The actual receipt and delivery of files is central to any solution. Common approaches to receiving and sending data within the EDI space include SFTP, encrypted data over standard FTP, and secure communications over AS2. BizTalk 2013 finally introduces native SFTP support. Historically, SFTP has been handled through third-party adapters. Dealing with encrypting and decrypting data on standard ports requires custom pipeline component code. Configuring AS2 for direct party-to-party communication requires certificates and complex configurations within BizTalk. This chapter will detail the setup and configuration for each of these methods, as well as how to successfully deliver various forms of EDI acknowledgements.

SFTP

SFTP is common option used in the exchange of data, since it ensures that the data is secure throughout the posting, storing, and retrieving stages. SFTP allows documents to be sent and received in plain text, as the protocol itself encrypts the information (with standard FTP, encrypting the file must be done through a custom pipeline component).

There are several options for sending and receiving data via SFTP in BizTalk Server. The first is the new SFTP native adapter that ships with BizTalk 2013. The second is the third-party bLogical BizTalk SFTP adapter (Blogical.Shared.Adapters.SFTP) available from CodePlex. Both of these adapters are covered here, as you may find that in some cases you may have connectivity challenges with certain SFTP servers. You will also find more robust scheduling options with the Blogical SFTP adapter.

Configuring the Native SFTP Adapter

With BizTalk 2013, the native support of SFTP is finally available. Prior to this release, only third-party (or custom) adapters could be used, but now you can set up SFTP communication as easily as standard FTP (which has been available natively since the beginning of BizTalk).

The available configurable properties on the adapter are different for inbound (receive) and outbound (send). The properties listed in the following sections come from both, and are intended to highlight the most important. Figure 5-1 shows the receive adapter properties.

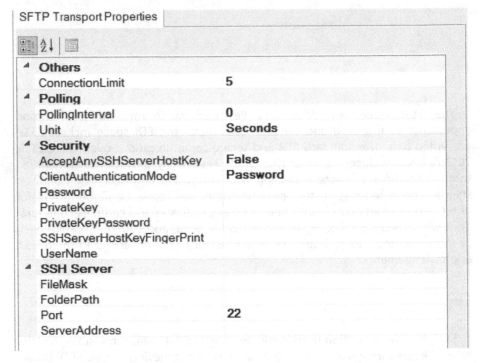

SFTP Transport Properties

▲ **Others**	
ConnectionLimit	**5**
▲ **Polling**	
PollingInterval	**0**
Unit	**Seconds**
▲ **Security**	
AcceptAnySSHServerHostKey	**False**
ClientAuthenticationMode	**Password**
Password	
PrivateKey	
PrivateKeyPassword	
SSHServerHostKeyFingerPrint	
UserName	
▲ **SSH Server**	
FileMask	
FolderPath	
Port	**22**
ServerAddress	

Figure5 -1. The receive adapter properties

> ■ **Note** Before you configure your SFTP adapter, make sure to test connectivity to the target SFTP site through a standard SFTP-compatible FTP utility (one excellent option is FileZilla, which has support for a wide array of FTP and SFTP connection types). There are a number of things that may require attention before you will be able to connect successfully, and it is much easier to trouble-shoot using a client utility than it is through the adapter.

ConnectionLimit

This field sets the number of concurrent connections to the target server. By default, this is 5. If you know that the possibility exists that you could have many concurrent connections to a single SFTP server, you will need to experiment with load testing and determine how you want to configure this field. It may be best to set this to 0 (no restrictions) and let the SFTP server manage how many connections it will allow (if it gets too many, it will throw an error back to BizTalk, and BizTalk can handle a retry of the data later).

PollingInterval and Unit

These fields are what you have available for setting a polling schedule. You can identify the polling interval; for example, if you want to check for files on the server every five minutes, you would set the PollingInterval to 5 and the Unit to Minutes. This is pretty limited functionality; if you need anything more robust, you will want to use the Blogical CodePlex adapter, covered later in this chapter.

AcceptAnySSHServerHostKey

This ensures that regardless of the key on the server, you will be able to make a connection. Because SFTP uses SSH, all communications require a key.

Password

Set this to the password used for connecting to the SFTP server.

FolderPath

If you are receiving data from a subdirectory of the SFTP site, you'll need to set the full path in this directory. Make sure to add a forward slash (/) before any path you enter in this property. The path is based off of the root server, so if your full path is 192.168.0.1/ChildOne/ChildTwo, you should enter /ChildOne/ChildTwo in this property, and enter 182.168.0.1 in the FolderPath property.

TargetFileName Property

The file name can be set using whatever combination of plain text and BizTalk macros that you may need. Some of the most common macros are shown in Table 5-1. Macros can be combined; if, for example, you want to show the source file name and combine it with the current datetime, you could put a value of %SourceFileName%_%datetime% in the SSH Remote File Name property.

Table5-1. Common BizTalk Macros

Macro	Description
%datetime%	This will create a string in the format of YYY-MM-DDThhmmss based on the current UTC time of the server. If you want to take into account the local time zone, you can use %datetime.tz%
%Message_ID%	Setting your target file name with this macro included in it ensures that you will always have a uniquely named file. The Message_ID is the GUID (Globally Unique Identifier) of the message in the BizTalk Message box.
%SourceFileName%	This will be set to the value available in the FILE.ReceivedFileName of the adapter picking up the original file. In some cases, you won't have access to the source file name in your send adapter, such as when the data is originating in an orchestration. This macro retains any file extensions that may have been present (such as .pgp or .txt).

There are more macros than are shown in this table, but there are some fairly severe limitations around what you can name files. If you find that the available BizTalk macros are not flexible enough to meet your requirements, you will have to develop a custom pipeline and pipeline component to create your filename. This pipeline can be added directly to the send pipeline on the SFTP send port.

UserName

Set this to the username used for connecting to the SFTP server.

Configuring the Blogical CodePlex SFTP Adapter

This adapter is available free of charge and is very reliable. It can be downloaded, compiled, and made available within BizTalk Server within a few minutes. It has been available for a number of years, and has some capabilities (like expanded scheduling) that make it more versatile than the new native SFTP adapter.

> ■ **Note** The SFTP adapter will automatically download the original host cer-
> tificate from the party with which you are interacting. However, if this certifi-
> cate expires (which is common), the SFTP adapter won't automatically be able
> to download the new certificate. If you get an exception in the Windows Event
> Log that says "HostKey does not match previously retrieved HostKey," you will
> need to browse to the `sftphostfiles.config` file and delete the HostKey
> setting. The directory where this file is located will be in the Local Settings of
> the host user that the SFTP adapter runs under. For example, if your BizTalk Host
> instance runs under `DOMAIN\Host_User_Account`, then you will browse to
> `Host_User_Account\Local Settings`. The config file will be buried un-
> der a unique directory several levels below, so you will likely need to run a search
> for it once you have located this directory.

Once the adapter has been installed, setting it up to receive and send data can
be done by creating a new receive location or send port and then setting the Type
property to SFTP (or whatever you named it during the installation). You can then
click Configure. You will want to configure the SFTP adapter with the key fields
shown in this section. In some cases, you will need to configure additional fields
than what is shown here, but in most cases these are all that is required.

Some of the properties listed (such as the Schedule) are unique to the receiving
of data. As you configure your SFTP send port or receive location, you'll be able to
easily identify which properties apply.

Schedule Property

This setting has some robust functionality for determining the schedule that the
source SFTP site will be queried. Clicking the ellipses on this property pops up an
interface that allows for scheduling on daily, weekly, monthly, or "timely" intervals.
You will most likely use the timely interval—every x number of minutes, for example. In Figure 5-2, you will see the property set to poll the source SFTP site every five
minutes. In most cases, you'll be pulling your EDI data on regular intervals throughout the day, but you'll need to coordinate with your trading partner to determine if
there are any scheduling windows that should be avoided.

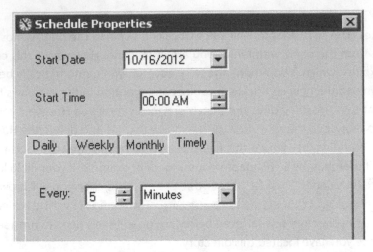

Figure5 -2. Setting the Schedule property for "timely" polling interval

After Get Property

This property defaults to Delete, which ensures that the file being retrieved is removed from the source SFTP site as soon as it has been successfully received by BizTalk. If there is an error in transmission, the file will remain on the server. In most cases, you will want to leave this set to Delete, but some trading partners provide archiving of data after a certain period of time, so you may want to leave the file on the server to take advantage of this. If this is not set to Delete, you will need to make sure your polling interval set in the Schedule property does not cause this same file to be retrieved multiple times before it is auto-archived by the trading partner.

SSH Error Threshold Property

The SSH Error Threshold property can be used to control how many errors can be encountered before the adapter shuts down. It is fairly common to have connectivity issues with SFTP sites, and it would make sense to increase this error threshold to a sizeable amount to account for this. If left at a low number, the adapter may shut down if the source site cannot be reached over a certain period of time.

> ■ **Note** If the SFTP adapter encounters errors, the exceptions will be logged to the Windows Event Viewer. Make sure to monitor the state of your SFTP ports, as they will automatically shut down if the error thresholds are exceeded.

SSH Host Property

This property should be set with the actual SFTP server host address. This could be an IP or a named server. It should only contain the root server name, not any subfolders. It should also not contain sftp://. An example of this property set to an IP would be 192.168.0.1.

SSH Port Property

The default port for SFTP servers is 22. If you are interacting with an SFTP server that has a different value, you will need to set the appropriate port value here.

SSH Password Property

Set this to the password used for connecting to the SFTP server.

SSH Remote Path Property

See the discussion on the FolderPath property in the section on the native SFTP adapter earlier in this chapter.

SSH Remote File Name Property

See the discussion on the TargetFileName property in the section on the native SFTP adapter earlier in this chapter.

SSH User Property

Set this to the username used for connecting to the SFTP server.

Trace Property

If you are running into exceptions when the SFTP adapter runs, you may want to set this property to True in order to log detailed information about what is happening.

Encrypted Data with Standard FTP

Using the standard FTP adapter to send and receive data with BizTalk is a breeze, but having to deal with encrypting and decrypting data is not. This section will outline the standard properties used to configure an FTP adapter for sending or receiving data. Additionally, it will discuss some of the challenges around custom pipeline and pipeline component development, and show how to set up a custom pipeline on a send port and a receive location.

Note All data sent/received using either of the SFTP adapters is automatically encrypted.

FTP Adapter Settings

If you are sending data over FTP, you can create a send port in BizTalk and set the Type to FTP. If you are receiving data over FTP, you can create a BizTalk receive location and set the Type to FTP. In either case, you will need to set the following key properties:

- **User Name:** The user with which you connect to the FTP site

- **Password:** The password used for connections

- **Server:** The FTP server. This should contain the IP or named server being connected to, and should not have the ftp:// prefix on it.

- **Port:** The specific port required for FTP connections

- **Folder:** The remote folder that you are posting data to. It should not have a leading forward slash (/) on it.

- **Representation:** Binary or ASCII. In general, this should be set to binary, but some FTP servers don't handle binary data, so you may have to experiment with settings here.

With the FTP adapter settings configured properly, you need only to focus on the requirements of the send pipeline.

Pipelines and Pipeline Components

One of the most complex tasks in BizTalk is creating custom pipelines, as it is pure C# development. If you are using PGP for encryption and decryption, some pointers on how to develop this custom pipeline component are outlined in this section. If you need to use an alternative encryption format, then you'll need to code something specific to the tools that are used for that format. In either case, you'll need someone who is familiar with C# development to work on this.

There are two items that must be set up for both the send pipeline that will encrypt data and the receive pipeline that will decrypt data. These items are the custom pipeline and the custom pipeline component. The custom pipeline component should be developed first. Let's assume that you are going to be dealing with PGP encrypted data. There are several tools that you could use; one of the easiest to interact with is GNU Privacy Guard (www.gnupg.org). This utility allows for the generation and management of PGP keys, and provides a command line interface that can be communicated with via C# .NET code.

Calling the command line tool requires that you build out a .NET class to wrap the call so that the pipeline can pass parameters to the command line and execute it (using System.Diagnostics.ProcessStartInfo is one option to do this). Assuming you have built a wrapper class for the GNU Privacy Guard command line tool (generally located in the GNU/GnuPG/pub directory), then a sample of calling this command line tool from within a custom pipeline component to encode data is shown In LIsting 5-1, while a sample of decoding data is shown in Listing 5-2.

Listing 5-1. Calling a Class to Encode Data with Parameters

```
GnuPGWrapper GPG = new GnuPGWrapper(_gnupgbindir);
GnuPGCommand GPGCommand = GPG.Command;
GPGCommand.Command = Commands.Encrypt;
GPGCommand.Recipient = _recipient;
// this is the recipient on the PGP key
GPGCommand.Passphrase = _passphrase ;
// this is the passphrase on the PGP key
GPGCommand.Armor = true;
GPGCommand.InputFile = inFile;
GPGCommand.OutputFile = outFile;
```

Listing 5-2. Calling a Class to Decode Data with Parameters

```
GnuPGWrapper GPG = new GnuPGWrapper(_gnupgbindir);
GnuPGCommand GPGCommand = GPG.Command;
GPGCommand.Command = Commands.Decrypt;
GPGCommand.InputFile = inFile;
GPGCommand.OutputFile = outFile;
GPGCommand.Passphrase = _passphrase;
// this is the passphrase of the PGP key
```

Creating the custom pipeline component will take some effort, and will depend on the encryption and decryption requirements of your solution. You will want to make a number of the fields configurable, so that you can use the send and receive pipelines on multiple trading partners. Figure 5-3 shows what these configurable properties could look like when they are set within the custom pipeline in Visual Studio.

Pipeline Component Properties	
EncryptData	True
GnuPGBinDir	C:\Program Files (x86)\GNU\GnuPG\bin
Passphrase	p@ssword1
Recipient	partnername@tradingpartner.com

Figure5 -3. Configurable parameters on the send pipeline component

The actual custom pipeline where you would be adding the custom pipeline components has to also be created. This is done within Visual Studio as a new BizTalk Pipeline project. An example of a send pipeline and what stage the custom pipeline component to encrypt should be added is shown in Figure 5-4. An example of a receive pipeline and the custom pipeline to decrypt is shown in Figure 5-5.

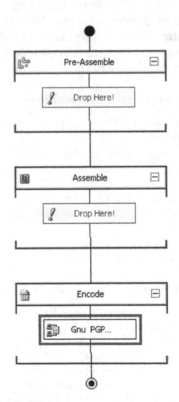

Figure5 -4. The send pipeline with encrypt component

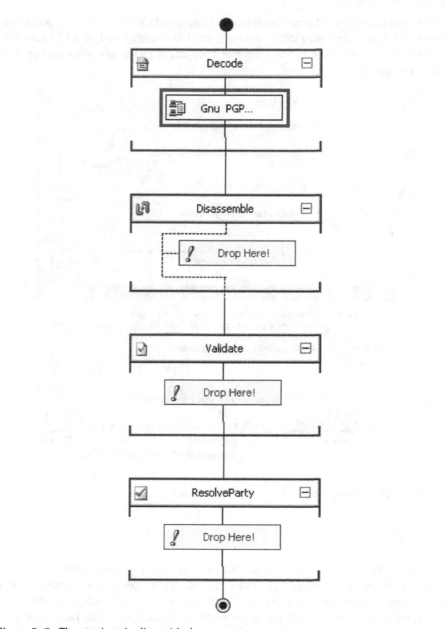

Figure5- 5. The receive pipeline with decrypt component

After you have created your pipelines and deployed them, they will be available to the send port and receive location where you have configured your FTP adapter. An example of a receive location with the decryption pipeline configured on it is shown in Figure 5-6.

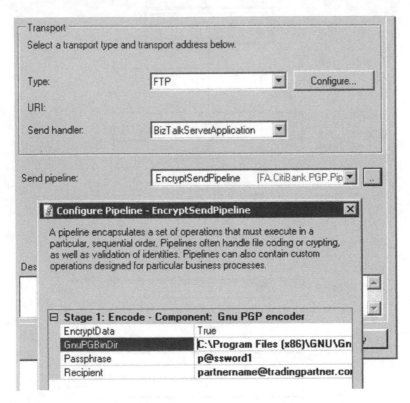

Figure5 -6. Configuring the pipeline on an FTP send port

AS2C ommunications

Configuring BizTalk for AS2 communications can be a time-consuming and difficult task. The most complex aspect of it is dealing with certificates. Both you and your trading partner are required to exchange certificates and configure communications with one another with the same settings. Should your data be encrypted? Should your MDN be signed? Do you have the correct certificate for the development environment vs. the production environment? Is your trading partner sending data in the expected format? The purpose of this section is to provide you with enough detail about configuring and testing AS2 so that you can avoid most of the pitfalls associated with setting this up.

Certificates

The first thing you will want to do is get your certificates set up. You'll begin by exchanging public keys with your trading partner. You should have a public and private key for your organization and a public key from the trading partner. Once you have these, you can take the following steps to set up the certificates on the BizTalk server.

CERTIFICATE CONFIGURATION FOR AS2

This exercise will demonstrate where to place and how to reference the certificates required in AS2 communications with BizTalk.

1. Log into the BizTalk server using a BizTalk service account.

2. Open the Certificate manager. From the Start Menu, click Run and type mmc. Once this is open, click File and select Add/Remove Snap-in. Select Certificates and click Add. Select the My user account option and click Finish. Select Certificates again and click Add; this time, select the Computer account option and click Next. Select the Local Computer option and click Finish. You should now have two certificate types, as shown in Figure 5-7. Once this is complete, click OK.

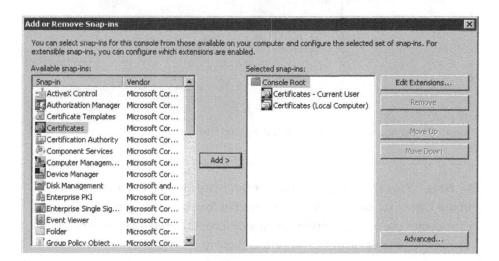

Figure5- 7. Configuring the certificate snap-in

3. With the Certificate console open, expand Certificates - Current User, and right-click Personal. Select Import and import the private key (.pfx) for your home organization.

4. Next, expand Certificates - Local Computer, and right-click Other People. Select Import and import the public key (.cer) for your trading partner's organization.

You should now see your certificates in several locations—the Personal and Other People folders of both the local computer and current user. With these certificates installed, you will now be able to reference them from the appropriate locations in BizTalk.

5. In the BizTalk Administration Console, right-click the BizTalk Group and select properties. Click the Certificate option and select Browse. Your home organization's certificate should appear; select it and click OK. Figure 5-8 shows the certificate set at this level. This will be your primary certificate used to sign outbound data.

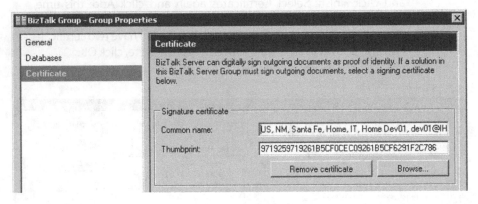

Figure5 -8. Configuring the certificate at the group level

Note You can override this default certificate for specific parties, if needed, in the Certificate page of the AS2 properties for your trading partner. In most cases, you'll use a single certificate for everyone, but there may be times when you'll need to use a unique certificate for signing.

6. Right-click your trading partner's BizTalk party in the BizTalk Admin Console's Parties folder and select properties. Click the Certificate option and click Browse. Select the trading partner's certificate.

There are only two other locations where you may need to configure certificates for your AS2 communications with a single trading partner: on the Signature Certificate page of the AS2 agreement (which allows for overriding the default home organization certificate on outbound documents and MDNs) and on any send ports that you may be using. However, it is unlikely that you will need to do anything with either of these if you are engaging in standard AS2 communications.

IIS and the BizTalk HTTP Receive Location

AS2 is communication over HTTP, so setting up a site within IIS on the BizTalk server is a requirement. There are a number of ways this can be set up, but the most common is to create a virtual directory for a specific trading partner that maps inbound requests to the BTSHTTPReceive.dll (which then pushes the inbound data to BizTalk for processing). This is a fairly involved yet easy configuration, and the following exercise outlines how to set up the various components.

> **Note** In some cases, your organization may not allow companies outside your network to post data directly via HTTP to BizTalk. In this case, you'll have to set up a proxy server to allow traffic to flow through your DMZ and hit the HTTP location in BizTalk. This is a separate area of expertise from BizTalk, and should be handled by a network administrator.

CONFIGURING IIS AND THE HTTP RECEIVE LOCATION

This exercise will demonstrate how to create and configure the appropriate IIS components to handle inbound AS2 posts. It will also show how to set up the BizTalk receive location that receives these posts.

1. Log into the BizTalk server using a BizTalk service account.

2. Open the IIS 7 manager, click the root server, and select the Handler Mappings option. In the Actions area on the right-hand side of the screen, click Add Script Map. Set the Request Path property to BtsHttpReceive.dll and set the Executable to the location of the BtsHttpReceive.dll (this is located in

the `HttpReceive` folder in the root BizTalk Server directory). Set the Name field to BizTalk HTTP Receive and then click the Request Restrictions button. In the Request Restrictions box, on the Access tab, select Script and click OK.

Click OK on the Add Script Map window when this has all been completed. Right-click the BizTalk HTTP Receive item that was just created and select Edit Feature Permissions. In the window that opens, select the Read, Script, and Execute boxes, and click OK.

See Figure 5-9 for a view of the final configuration.

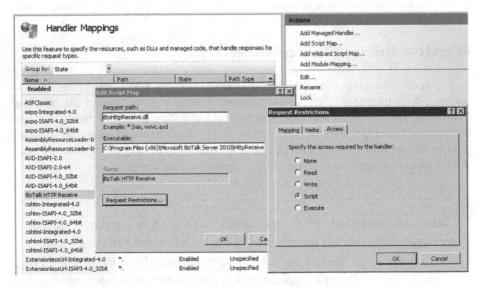

Figure5 -9. Configuring the HTTP receive handler map in IIS

3. Back on the root server in IIS, click the ISAPI and CGI Restrictions icon. In the window that opens, set the BTSHTTPReceive Restriction setting to Allowed, as shown in Figure 5-10.

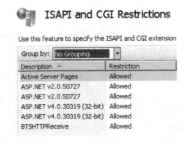

Figure5 -10. More configuring of the HTTP receive handler map in IIS

4. Create a new Application Pool in IIS, and set the name to BizTalkAppPool (or similar). Set the .NET Framework Version property to 4.0 (whichever specific version is available to you) and the Managed Pipeline mode to Integrated.

5. Create a new virtual directory (as an application) under the default web site. The name of this site should be specific to the trading partner that you will be receiving data from over HTTP, so in this case name it TradingPartner. Set the Application Pool to the app pool you created in the previous step and select Test Connection to ensure you are able to connect.

> ■ **Note** Depending on your security setting, you may find that you also need to set the physical path credentials to a specific account that has access to that directory. The easiest way to access this is to right-click the web application you created and select Manage Application and then Advanced Settings.

6. Click the virtual directory you just created and select the Authentication icon. In Authentication window that opens, set Anonymous Authentication to Enabled.

This completes the setup of all IIS-related components for AS2. If additional trading partners need to be set up, create one additional virtual directory for each one.

Agreements and Party Settings

In order to specify how to handle the AS2 data and how to work with the underlying EDI document that is being sent via AS2, you will need to set up a BizTalk party and two agreements. One agreement is for the AS2 messaging, and one agreement is for dealing with the actual EDI data. The basic steps for setup are as follows for receiving AS2 data from a trading partner (sending data to a trading partner is very similar):

- Create a new BizTalk party with the name of the trading partner from which you will be receiving data.

- If you will be sending a 997 to the trading partner, specify the send port that the 997 will be sent out on.

- Create a new agreement on this party that will handle AS2 messaging (you can call it something like Agreement_AS2).
  - On the General tab, set the Protocol property to AS2, the First Party to the trading partner, and the Second Party to your home organization. Once you've set the General tab this way, two additional tabs will appear: one for inbound data from the trading partner, and one for outbound data to the trading partner. If you are just receiving data from the trading partner and returning an MDN, you only need to configure the inbound trading partner tab.
  - On the inbound trading partner tab, on the Identifiers tab, set the AS2-From and AS2-To properties to the appropriate values as defined in your trading partner agreement. These must match what is on the AS2 envelope being sent to you. Figure 5-11 shows an example of these settings.

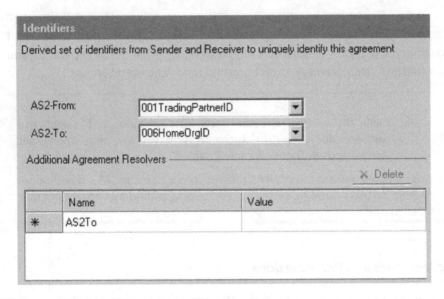

Figure5 -11. The Identifiers tab in the AS2 agreement

  - On the Validation tab for the AS2 agreement, you can set the appropriate values for validation of the data. For example, if you are receiving a signed and encrypted inbound post from a trading partner, then you would set the properties as shown in Figure 5-12.

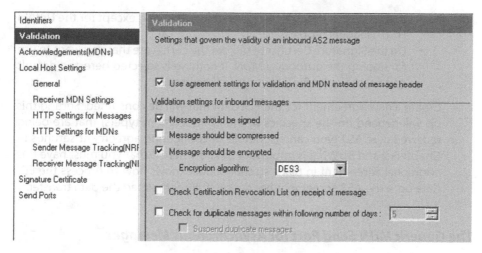

Figure5- 12. The Validation tab in the AS2 agreement

   ° On the Acknowledgement tab of the AS2 agreement, you can set the properties that pertain to the MDN response back to the trading partner. If you need to send an unsigned MDN, you can use the properties shown in Figure 5-13. If you are sending a signed MDN, then the certificate specific in the Signature Certificate settings will be used (or, if none is specified, then the default certificate associated with the BizTalk group will be used).

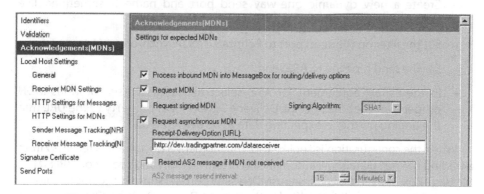

Figure5- 13. The Acknowledgement tab in the AS2 agreement

   ° There are some additional properties that will likely need to be set or adjusted on the other tabs; a few of the most common are noted here.
- On the Receive MDN Settings tab, enable the Sign Requested MDN setting if you want to always send an MDN, regardless of what is noted on the inbound AS2 request from the trading partner.
- In the HTTP Settings for Messages, enable everything except for the Ignore SSL Certificate Name Mismatch property.

- In the HTTP Settings for MDN, enable everything except for the Unfold HTTP Headers property.
- On the Signature Certificate tab, set the certificate that you want to use for signing the outbound MDN. If nothing is selected here, the default certificate for the BizTalk group will be used.

- Create a new agreement for the EDI data that will be consumed. Setting this up will depend on the specifics of the EDI document type(s) that are being received over AS2 (you can see details of configuring agreement settings in Chapters 2 and 3). What is important to know here is that you must have this additional agreement in place so that BizTalk knows how to process the EDI data once the AS2 agreement has successfully completed the data transfer.

The Generic MDN Send Port for Asynchronous Messages

The MDN is the acknowledgement for AS2 posts. There are two possible methods for postback of an MDN: synchronous and asynchronous. The synchronous response is posted back via the same open HTTP connection that the original document came in on, and does not require any additional BizTalk components (simply set the Request MDN checkbox in the BizTalk agreement, and it will automatically post back). For asynchronous MDNs, a send port must be created. You can create a generic send port that will work for all parties by taking the following steps.

- Create a new dynamic one-way send port and name it something like SendAsyncronousMDNs.

- Set the filter on the send port to EdiIntAS.IsAS2AsynchronousMdn == True.

- Set the send pipeline to AS2Send.

- In the BizTalk agreement for AS2, select the Request Asynchronous MDN property and set the Receipt-Delivery-Option (URL) property to the URL that the trading partner is expecting data to be delivered on.

When the configuration is set like this, the moment a document is received from a trading partner, BizTalk will automatically create an MDN and drop it on the BizTalk Message Box. The SendAsynchronousMDNs send port will subscribe to this document and send it out to the URL specified in the Receipt-Deliver-Option (URL) property on whatever trading partner's agreement was just used to receive the data.

Testing your AS2 Configuration

One of the most challenging (and frustrating) aspects of AS2 configuration is the actual trading partner testing. The best advice is to plan to set up your AS2 configuration in stages. Try to exchange plain text data (unencrypted and unsigned) first before dealing with the various settings requiring certificates. If you can get the plain, unencoded data to flow (and the MDN to return) successfully, then you can move into testing encryption and signing.

There are many things that can go wrong during testing, and the error messages are often very generic and cryptic. The errors could be on your side, or they could be on the trading partner's side. The more you can do to limit what is being tested at any given stage, the quicker you will be able to get to resolution and completion.

Sending 997/999 Acknowledgements

There are several types of acknowledgements that can be sent in response to EDI communications: functional (997/999), technical (TA), and MDNs (for AS2). Configuring and sending MDN acknowledgements was covered earlier in the AS2 section in this chapter. Technical acknowledgements are rarely required, and are identical in setup to the functional ones. You will now look at sending the functional acknowledgements for the EDI data itself. The steps to take are as follows.

- Open the BizTalk party agreement that relates to the documents and trading partner that you need to set up the functional acknowledgement for, and click the Acknowledgements tab. You will be able to set a checkbox next to 997 Expected, as shown in Figure 5-14.

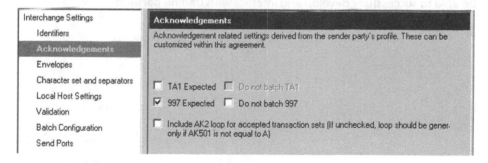

Figure5-14. The Acknowledgement tab in the EDI agreement

- Set up one send port per trading partner. These send ports will subscribe directly to the BizTalk Message Box, and will filter on the specific trading partner required. The send port should have the following settings:
  - The Transport type, which is FTP, SFTP, or other. Set the appropriate connection information for the actual adapter that will be used to connect to the trading partner.
  - The send pipeline should be set to EdiSend or, if you are required to encrypt 997 data (which is uncommon), you will need to add your custom send pipeline to do the encryption.

- ° Three filters, as follows:
- ° EDI.IsSystemGeneratedAck == true
  - EDI.ST01 == 997 (or 999 if version 5010)
  - EDI.ISA06 == [this should be the specific trading partner's ID that you are configuring for this specific send port; this ID can be retrieved from the Party settings of the BizTalk agreement where you have configured 997s to be sent]

- Depending on your configuration, you may need to associated the 997/999 send port with your agreement on the Send Ports tab.

Once you have these settings configured, BizTalk will automatically generate a 997/999 when the inbound EDI document is received and drop it on the BizTalk Message Box. Next, the send port will pick it up and deliver it to the specified destination.

Conclusion

This chapter has gone into depth on the most common transport mechanisms for any BizTalk EDI health care implementation you may need to build out. It has also shown how to deal with 997/999s and MDN acknowledgements. With the information related to AS2, SFTP, and encrypted data over FTP that has been covered, you'll be able to successfully develop and interact with trading partners.

Index

◼ T, U

◼ V, W, X, Y, Z